A PASSION FOR GOD

A Passion for God

Reflections on the Gospels
Volume Three

John Michael Talbot

Servant Publications
Ann Arbor, Michigan

Cover design by Michael Andaloro
Cover photograph by Mark Tucker

Published by Servant Publications
P.O. Box 8617
Ann Arbor, Michigan 48107

91 92 93 94 10 9 8 7 6 5 4 3 2 1

Printed in the United States of America
ISBN 0-89283-705-5

Library of Congress Cataloging-in-Publication Data
(Revised for volume 3)
Talbot, John Michael.
  Reflections on the Gospels.
  1. Bible. N.T. Gospel—Meditations.   I. Title.
BS2555.4.T35 1986 242′.3   86-206812
ISBN 0-89283-306-8 (v. 1)

Contents

Note to the Reader

APASSION FOR GOD is designed to help the reader meditate on a Gospel passage thoughout the day. Some readers will be particularly interested to note that the readings correspond to the daily Gospel readings for the liturgical year. This third volume in the *Reflections on the Gospels* series covers the first week through the sixth week of Ordinary Time, the Lenten Season, and the Easter Season. The second volume in the series covers the seventh week through the twenty-first week of Ordinary Time, while volume one begins with the twenty-second week and continues through the Advent and Christmas Seasons. The particular week and day of the readings in this volume are indicated at the beginning of each reflection. For example, (4: Monday) indicates that the reading is the Gospel text for Monday of the fourth week of Ordinary Time. Thus, this volume and the other two can be read in concert with the liturgical seasons. Whether or not you read it in this way, it is designed to bring you into contact every day with the living Word of God.

Preface

THE 1990S ARE BEING CALLED the "Decade of Evangelization." It is a time when many are hearing the prophetic word to "get back to basics," to "rekindle the fire," and to "return to the first love." It is a time to return to the radical simplicity of the gospel of Jesus Christ.

As I have traveled around the country with the ministry team of my community, the Brothers and Sisters of Charity, we have proclaimed this message time after time. In praise and worship, we have seen an anointing of the Spirit that has inspired an enthusiasm largely unseen since the late 1960s and the early 1970s. In preaching we have seen a radical gospel challenge to follow Jesus that makes some uncomfortable, but it has prompted thousands upon thousands of others to stand on their feet and come forward in order to respond as willing disciples.

This book is a collection of my morning teachings and messages to the community which God has used me to found, the Brothers and Sisters of Charity. Ironically, these teachings were given at a time when we ourselves were going through great spiritual battle. Like everyone else, we must battle against the almost irresistible allurements of American society. We fight allurements of materialism with gospel poverty. The rampant sexual promiscuity of the West is fought by our covenant of single, celibate, or marital chastity. The undue individualism that so threatens any corporate structure of society—the family, Christian community, the church, or even the work force—is overcome by our covenant of obedience.

Of course, the subtle spiritual deception of the New Age movement is also a constant threat. When it can't come in the front door, it tries to sneak in the back door. Many programs that may be good when approached properly, threaten to take our eyes off of Jesus and to place them on ourselves. Enneagrams, twelve-step programs, and pseudo-psychological analysis seem to be in vogue everywhere. We are quick to center on self rather than on Jesus, and quick to blame someone else for our "dysfunction."

I believe there are two major danger signals to watch for in any spiritual program. First, does it sidetrack us from placing Jesus and Jesus alone at the center of everything we are about? Second, does it bring in a kind of self-indulgence in the name of "self-awareness," rather than the real self-sacrifice of Jesus? No matter how good the program, if this is the fruit, it is not being carried out in the real Spirit of God.

The following teachings were given at a time when our community was in the throes of just such a battle. The message was strongly resisted by some, and was accepted by others. Those who persisted in their resistance finally chose to leave. Those who "fought the good fight" were able to stay and build towards the future. Unfortunately, some of God's "little ones" grew confused and disoriented and were lost as casualties along the way.

As we face the 1990s, I believe it is only by radically refocusing on the simple gospel of Jesus Christ that we will be able to truly make this the "Decade of Evangelization." It may not lead us to the success we imagine. It may lead us only to the cross. We may actually be privileged enough to evoke the same response as Jesus did in his own day. Then will our words and our work be fully Christian.

It is my prayer these teachings do the same for you as they did for my community. May they enflame you with with a passion for God alone. May they challenge you to make a choice. Then you will know if you have really accepted the challenge to evangelize the world in the name of Jesus Christ.

Part I

Ordinary Time

Radically Change
Mark 1:14-20 (1:Monday)

"Come after me; I will make you fishers of men." They immediately abandoned their nets and became his followers. vv. 17, 18

There are many challenges that threaten the very existence of modern civilization. Rampant materialism, the militarism of the arms race, the holocaust of abortion, and the breakdown of the nuclear family are some of the more obvious ones. Many Christian leaders believe we are heading for another Dark Age. The outlook is not good if there is not a radical change in our whole way of life.

Today's Gospel calls us to that change. The call went forth to everyday people like you and me. Simon Peter was a family man with a good fishing business. He knew well the normal responsibilities of being a husband and a father. No doubt, he also knew the feeling of being trapped into a system of society that would never allow him to break free.

Jesus calls Simon Peter to change today. He gives him the opportunity to radically change his whole way of life. Simon Peter and Andrew have the courage to respond. They immediately abandon their business to be about the business of Jesus Christ.

You say that you cannot change radically. You have a good job. You have a business. You have a family to think about. So did Simon Peter! But because he had the courage and faith to respond, Jesus raised him up as the leader of the church and entrusted him with the keys of the kingdom. He got back more than he could possibly imagine. He also got the opportunity to become a martyr for Christ.

If you have the courage and faith to respond in a similar way, Jesus will also give you a whole new way of life that far exceeds your wildest dreams. That doesn't necessarily mean that Jesus will call you to leave your business, spouse, or children. But he will set you free to do great things in building God's kingdom. He will also give you many opportunities to be crucified with him.

Where are the Simon Peters today? Who will be willing to change radically in order to meet the awesome challenges of our modern world with the answers that only Jesus can give? Is it you? Come and follow Jesus. Leave your boats and nets at the shore and walk in the poverty, the peace, the purity, and the perseverence of Christ. Then you will do your part to solve the world's problems. □

Dealing with Demons
Mark 1:21-28 (1:Tuesday)

There appeared in their synagogue a man with an unclean spirit.

v. 23

Demons are a popular topic in many Christian circles nowadays. In fact, many Christians spend so much time talking about "warfare," they often forget to talk about love. We can become so concerned about Satan that we often take our eyes off of Jesus!

What is the correct approach to Satan, devils, and demons? Most of Jesus' healing ministry did not include any mention of demons. He heals in response to faith (Mt 8:5-13; 9:2, 22-29), forgiveness (Lk 5:20), and love (Lk 7:47, 50). Sometimes it was simply because of the power of God within him (Lk 5:17) or to reveal his own power and authority (Lk 5:24). Contrary to the teaching of many popular preachers today, demons are not connected with every sickness or every healing.

However, today's Gospel points out that deliverance from evil spirits was a definite part of Jesus' ministry. Jesus gave the authority of this deliverance ministry to the twelve apostles (Lk 9:1), the seventy-two disciples (Lk 10:17), and to all who profess faith in Christ (Mk 16:17). As St. Paul says,

"Our battle is not against human forces but against the principalities and powers, the rulers of this world of darkness, the evil spirits in regions above" (Eph 6:12). Spiritual warfare is real!

Many say that Satan, the devil, and demons are not real, that they were only the way for the people of old to express the mysteries we have now unlocked by modern psychology and science. This is to some degree true, but the clear teaching of Jesus in the Scriptures and through the church is that demons do exist as personal spiritual beings, as does their leader, Satan.

How does Jesus deal with demons? Jesus had authority to "rebuke them sharply," to command them to be silent, and to order them to depart from the possessed person (Mk 1:25). He commanded the demons to name themselves and he could send them where he chose after commanding them out of a person (Mk 5:1-15). He also overcame personal temptation through a correct understanding of God's Word in Scripture, not to mention his own preparation in the desert through solitude, fasting, and prayer (Mt 4:1-11). Finally, he warned that deliverance is not enough without filling the empty place left behind with the presence of God (Mt 12:43-45).

We, too, are to take authority over demons of darkness in our lives and in the lives of others. We must only do this in Jesus' name (Mk 16:17; Jude 9). This is, for instance, the way St. Paul delivered the clairvoyant slave girl in Philippi (Acts 11:18). We must not assume, however, that the use of his name is like some magical incantation or sorcery. It must be accompanied by real Christian living, genuine imitation of Christ.

Remember when the Jewish exorcists said to the demon, "I adjure you by the Jesus whom Paul preaches," the demon answered, "Jesus I recognize, Paul I know; but who are you?" The evil spirit then overpowered them, leaving them "naked and bruised" (Acts 19:15-16). Furthermore, even in the case of the apostles already commissioned by Jesus to expel demons, sometimes they could not expel the demons without "prayer and fasting" (Mk 9:14-29). Demonology is nothing to be toyed with. It is real and must be dealt with seriously. It must be accompanied by serious Christian living. Otherwise, it will miscarry and fail. □

Family Matters
Mark 1:29-39 (1:Wednesday)

He entered the house of Simon and Andrew with James and John. Simon's mother-in-law lay ill with a fever ... He went over to her ... and the fever left her. vv. 29-31

How do we bring the healing ministry of Jesus to our own families, the ones we love, and those closest to us? Oh yes, it is easy to have a "healing ministry" when we deal with those we will never see again or see rarely. What about those we see every day? This daily contact keeps such healing ministries honest.

Jesus went right into the family of Simon Peter and healed. Scholars say that Peter's house in Capernaum became a kind of base from which Jesus worked. Jesus stayed in the area of Galilee and was known both in Capernaum and in the surrounding villages through daily contact. As yesterday's Gospel said, "From that point on his reputation spread throughout the surrounding region of Galilee."

This is not to assume that response to Jesus was always positive. He was first rejected in his home town of Nazareth where he said, "No prophet gains acceptance in his native place" (Lk 4:23-30). They tried to kill him at Nazareth! As

Mark says, "He could work no miracle there, . . . so much did their lack of faith distress him" (Mk 6:5, 6). When Jesus ministered to the point of depriving himself of food, his own family said, "He is out of his mind" (Mk 3:21). Also, "he began to reproach the towns where most of his miracles had been worked, with their failure to reform" (Mt 11:20). These towns were Chorazin, Bethsaida, and Capernaum. The last is the very town where he healed Peter's mother-in-law!

Apparently, Jesus didn't expect or promise great success with our own families, but that didn't keep him from ministering to those closest to himself and his disciples. He gave them every opportunity to accept his ministry. He had the courage to stay close enough to sometimes see real results of his own powerful ministry.

Perhaps this is why the early Christians asked a bishop or deacon to be "a good manager of his own household" (1 Tm 3:1-13). Even in the case where the whole family does not share faith in Christ, they are encouraged to stay together, unless "the unbeliever wishes to separate" (1 Cor 7:12-16). Concerning the care of widows, Paul says, "If anyone does not provide for his own relatives and especially for members of his immediate family, he has denied the faith; he is worse than an unbeliever" (1 Tm 5:8). No doubt, even in the midst of domestic misunderstanding, the early Christians placed a high priority on the value of the family, as well as on the family of God.

How do we minister our own gifts in the midst of our own family and friends? Are we bold and effective among strangers, and ineffective at home? Are we willing to face the possibility that we may be causing a lack of real anointing on our life and ministry by our unwillingness to minister in the accountable setting of our own family and church home? Finally, how do we deal with failure at home? Do we become angry and upset, or do we simply continue in the sure and steady love of Jesus? □

Jesus Wills Wellness
Mark 1:40-45 (1:Thursday)

I will do it. Be cured.... Go off and present yourself to the priest and offer for your cure what Moses prescribed. That should be a proof for them. vv. 41, 44

Do we really believe Jesus can or wants to heal us of our sickness? How does that relate to the sacraments of the church?

Today's Gospel answers the first question in the person of the leper: "I will do it. Be cured." In all of the Gospels we never see Jesus refusing to cure anyone! In Capernaum "he could work no miracle there so much did their lack of faith distress him," but even then the text makes the provision, "apart from curing a few who were sick by laying hands on them" (Mk 6:5, 6). True enough, Jesus once denied the request of the people of Capernaum not to leave in order to minister in other towns, but this was only after, "All who had people sick with a variety of diseases took them to him, and he laid hands on each of them and cured them" (Lk 4:40-44). In all Scripture Jesus never refused to heal anyone!

In fact, healing was one of the main ways to describe Jesus' ministry. "Go back and report . . . what you see and hear: the blind recover their sight, cripples walk, lepers are cured, the deaf hear, dead men are raised to life, and the poor have the good news preached to them" (Mt 11:4, 5). Notice, healing was a priority in Jesus' ministry.

Today's Gospel also points out that there was no immediate conflict between the healings of Jesus and the established institutional religion of the Jews in the law of Moses. The same thing can be said more assuredly regarding the overt Christian expressions of institutional religion. St. James says, "Is there anyone sick among you? He should ask for the presbyters of the church. They in turn are to pray over him, anointing him with oil in the Name (of the Lord). This prayer uttered in faith will reclaim the one who is ill, and the Lord will restore him to health. If he has committed any sins, forgiveness will be his. Hence, declare your sins to one another, and pray for one another, that you may find healing" (Jas 5:14-16). This is the scriptural base for the sacrament of the anointing of the sick.

Furthermore, St. Paul says in reverse logic that the reason "why many among you are sick and infirm, and why so many are dying" is that many receive Eucharist or the Lord's Supper unworthily and "sin against the body and blood of the Lord" by not "recognizing the body" (1 Cor 11:27-31). Therefore, the duly administered sacraments of the church bring healing, while abuse of them brings sickness.

Yet the healing of Jesus in the church is not limited to church leadership and sacramental remedies. Jesus says, "Signs like these will accompany those who have professed their faith . . . they will be able to drink deadly poison without harm, and the sick upon whom they lay their hands will recover" (Mk 16:17-18). This promise of being healed and healing is for "those who have professed their faith," not just for an elite few.

This healing ministry is not the result of clever words or sacred knowledge. It is the result of faith, love, and the power of God. As Jesus says, "If you are ready to believe that you will receive whatever you ask for in prayer, it shall be done for you" (Mk 11:24). There is no great secret to divine healing. You simply step out in love and faith and let Jesus take care of the rest. □

Please, Interrupt!
Mark 2:1-12 (1:Friday)

While he was delivering God's word to them, some people arrived bringing a paralyzed man to him. v. 3

How do we respond when our normal church services are interrupted? Jesus is preaching. He is delivering the Word of

God. Suddenly it is obvious that a paralytic is being brought in. It is what many of us would consider an "interruption." How does Jesus respond?

Jesus does not have the man put into a special section for the "handicapped," nor does he put people off until the end of the service. He heals the man on the spot. He also uses this opportunity to address a deeper issue: his authority to forgive sins.

Notice that Jesus doesn't heal the man first. No! He offers the man the forgiveness of his sins. Many times lack of forgiveness will foster hurt and anger that can, themselves, manifest in physical sickness. Jesus speaks to the core problem here. He doesn't just heal him physically. He first does a surgery in his soul. He forgives him his sins.

Also notice that the faith to which Jesus responds is not the faith of the paralytic. It is the faith of those who carried him to Jesus. The forgiveness of our sins is not an isolated thing, only between ourselves and God. It affects other people. Consequently, other people can have an effect on this process through their own faithful intercession.

Last comes the physical healing. It is the least important part of today's story, but it is not unimportant. Jesus does heal the paralytic, to prove that he has the authority to forgive sins and heal the sickness of the soul. The Jews of old held that only God could forgive sins. Jesus is now exercising this divine power and granting forgiveness from sin to all who will turn to him.

Do we accept this wonderful gift from God in our life? Are we willing to seek a deeper healing, or do we settle for a superficial one? Do we recognize our interdependence on others in this process of forgiveness? Finally, are we willing to interrupt our agenda in order to bring healing to others? Our priority might even be a church service or liturgy. It might be our private schedule for prayer, study, or work. Let God interrupt your life today. Let him forgive you and heal you. Let him have full authority in your life. □

Leaving the Past
Mark 2:13-17 (1:Saturday)

"Follow me." Levi got up and became his follower. While Jesus was reclining to eat in Levi's house . . . vv. 14-15

We are called to radically follow Jesus. In the face of the rampant materialism of the West, we are especially called to divest ourselves of unnecessary possessions and embrace gospel poverty. We are also called to break with peer groups that pressure us into continual sin. Before we get too excited about "throwing it all away," we had best look more closely at how this was done by the apostles.

Levi, or Matthew, was a tax collector. He was very much wrapped up in the materialism of his day. Tax collectors were notorious for cheating their own people and getting rich in the process. They were also notorious for hanging out with a very loose-living crowd of people.

In today's Gospel Levi gets right up from his tax collector's table to respond to Jesus' call to discipleship. He leaves everything on the spot. This could lead us to the conclusion that Levi left all his possessions and his job for good.

Yet look at the rest of the text: we next find Jesus in Levi's (or Matthew's) house at a large dinner. Who paid for it? Probably Levi! Furthermore, the house is filled with Levi's old friends, probably not a church-going crowd. They were fellow tax collectors, drunks, and prostitutes. On one hand, it could be argued that Levi "left everything" to become Jesus' follower. On the other hand, we find him back in the midst of his possessions and old friends immediately after his conversion to Christ.

There are many possible explanations for this. It might well have been one last good-bye to his old way of life to show Jesus to his old friends before embarking on his new life as a disciple. At the very least, it was an attempt for Levi to bring Jesus to those still trapped in the sinful way of life out of which Jesus had called him.

Looking at similar situations in the lives of the other apostles such as Simon Peter, whose mother-in-law Jesus visited, indicating Simon still had contact with family and friends after following Jesus. Just so it is probable that Levi gave up his job as a tax collector, but did not totally give up his house, family, or friends. He probably helped bring them to Christ as well.

Do we totally open up our house to Jesus, or do we keep certain parts for ourselves? Do we really reach out to those closest to us who are in need of Jesus? Lastly, are we willing to lay aside our own "tax business," our pursuits that are inconsistent with the radical call of the gospel? Jesus calls us all today. Like Levi, we are called to a response that helps bring Jesus to those who are most in need. □

New Skins for Wine
Mark 2:18-22 (2:Monday)

No man pours new wine into old wineskins. . . . No, new wine is poured into new skins. v. 22

How does the current renewal of the Spirit fit into the older existing movements and structures of the church? There is often tension about how to fit a new movement, raised up by the Spirit, into the church. Too much conformity of the new to the old will destroy the uniqueness of the new. While too much rigidity on the part of the new towards the old will cause it to degenerate into self-righteousness.

Jesus and the apostles face a similar question today. They are being compared to the practice of another "renewal" group, John the Baptist and his disciples, but they are really being compared to the more established renewal group in Israel: the Pharisees. The apparent issue was the practice of fasting. Yet Jesus gives us an answer that applies to all customs and practices of religion. He tells us you cannot sew a patch of unshrunken cloth on an old cloak or put new wine into an old wineskin. If you try to do so, you will end up destroying both.

Jesus does not go so far as to say that old wine or old wineskins are bad. Neither does he say that the old cloak is bad. Quite the contrary! Old wine is always sought after as the best wine. Likewise, there is nothing quite so comfortable as an old cloak. It is just a bad thing to try to artificially force a new movement into old categories. The new movement may not initially appear to be as good, but may end up better than the old, given time.

Throughout the history of the church, the Spirit has raised up new communities and movements under various founders. The above process always applies. They must always be given the freedom by the church to develop their own "wineskins," without being forced into the old. Likewise, they must respectfully recognize that the older movements have much to teach us.

Do we stifle the Spirit by trying to put new wine into old wineskins? Do we sin through pride by not recognizing that the old wine is in many ways better than the new? Do we sin through pride by not admitting that the new may someday be better than the old? These are the questions we must face if any new movement is to really be consistent with the words of Jesus Christ. □

Packaged Religion
Mark 2:23-28 (2:Tuesday)

Have you never read what David did when he was in need and he and his men were hungry? How he entered God's house . . . and ate the holy bread which only the priests were permitted to eat? He even gave it to his men. vv. 25-26

Today Jesus is taking one of those uncomfortable passages of Scripture and causing the religious leaders of his day to come to grips with it. It is the nature of any organized religion to try to keep the work of God in a nice, neat package. For every work of God there is a place. There are doctrines, sacramental rituals, and structures. All is kept very balanced and safe.

While there is nothing wrong with organized religion, and God does in fact work through these various religious categories, God is not limited to them. God may raise up these things as gifts and tools for his grace, but the Giver is above the gifts. The Craftsman is above his tools.

The Old Testament is very clear about the ministry of the priest. It teaches that any lay person who tries to usurp the function of the priest is to be put to death. It is considered a sin of major moral consequence. Yet David, a layman, eats the holy bread that only a priest may eat.

There are some important points here (1 Sm 21). David did this in union with the instruction of the priest. What he does is irregular, but it is not rebellious. There is a reverence maintained both for the ordained priesthood and the holy bread. Yet a very real need on the part of David, the Lord's anointed, is met.

Similar issues face the modern church. There is a growing crisis concerning the number of ordained clergy and the proportionate needs of the laity. More and more the church is attempting to meet those needs by the participation of qualified laity in ministry. In areas where there is no ordained clerical leadership, this even involves participation in preaching God's word and administering some sacraments. Of course, this is always done in union with the local bishop, while maintaining a due respect and reverence for the unique ministry of the ordained clergy, the Word of God, and the sacraments. In areas where this reality is widespread, such as the Third World, the church has continued to flourish with perhaps an even greater vibrance.

Are we flexible in our approach to liturgy and sacraments? Do we allow Jesus to meet the needs of the people in whatever way he desires? Conversely, are we really respectful of the ordained clerical leadership and their unique call to preach God's Word and administer the sacraments? If the church is too rigid, she will force her people into revolt. If the people are not really respectful of the leadership and sacraments of the church, they run the risk of rebelling against God and facing spiritual death. Where are you in this balance? □

Be Angry, Sin Not
Mark 3:1-6 (2:Wednesday)

He looked around at them with anger, for he was deeply grieved that they had closed their minds against him. v. 5

Anger can be a destructive thing, but the repression of anger can be even more destructive. Sometimes it is even the will of God that anger be acted upon and voiced. Both viewpoints must be explored.

James tells us clearly that the anger of men does not work the righteousness of God (Jas 1:20). We know all too well of the instances where outbursts of anger have broken relationships between individuals, communities, and even nations. Jesus speaks clearly against anger. He explicitly says it is the root cause behind abusive words and implies that it lies at the heart of violence and war. The wisdom literature of the Old Testament proclaimed long ago the findings of modern science when it said that anger brings broken relationships, war, sickness, and even death. This kind of anger is clearly not a work of God.

This does not mean that there isn't a godly anger. Jesus is angry today at sin in the Church and in the world. Paul tells us, "If you are angry, let it be without sin" (Eph 4:26). God himself has an anger. Needless to say, this is not sin.

First, we must remember that emotions are neither good nor bad; it is what we do with emotion that makes them good or bad. Anger is not bad in and of itself. What we do with it determines whether it is good or bad. To leave it uncontrolled is never good. The energy of anger should never be repressed. Doing this is like pushing down on a spring. Sooner or later it will let go with an even greater force.

The energy of anger needs to be channeled. Anger needs to be rechanneled into love or directed against sin. Usually we follow the axiom, "Love the sinner, hate the sin." Anger at sin is appropriate, but anger at people can be more dangerous. Furthermore, the sheer energy of anger can usually be redirected into an equal energy of love. Love is a decision.

Today Jesus is angry, and he is angry with people because of their sins! Sometimes it is okay to be angry with people. It can lead to healing. Don't try to ignore this reality. Anger is!

Don't repress it. Own it. Say, "you are making me angry." Once you do this, then you can decide what to do about it in a way that leads to healing. If you give yourself and others the permission to be angry without making a moral judgment about the anger itself, then you can go on to work out the moral issues without repressing the anger. Repression will cause the anger to explode. Anger expressed moderately is far more healthy.

It is like the fault line around an earthquake. If you never relieve the pressure in small ways, a major earthquake will result. If you relieve the pressure as it comes, bit by bit, then a major earthquake can be avoided. The same is true with anger. If you express anger as it comes, you can avoid a big explosion. If you repress it when it comes, then an earthquake is on the way!

Do we know how to get angry as Jesus did? Do we know how to acknowledge it and work through it? Or do we deny it and repress it in an attempt to be like the stereotype of Jesus, meek and mild? Be like the real Jesus who got angry with those who had hardened their minds and hearts to God. Learn how to get angry in a godly way. Then you will avoid the anger that is ungodly. □

Beware of Superficiality
Mark 3:7-12 (2:Thursday)

He kept ordering them sternly not to reveal who he was. v. 12

How different from our modern sales approach! Even in ministry, the modern approach is to "blow your own horn" in order to drum up business. Ministries often spend huge amounts on advertising, or else there would be no one to hear the message. Many resort to almost any means of advertising in order to get the word out.

Jesus' approach is different. He doesn't want cheap publicity. When demons start loudly proclaiming him, he silences them. Even though what they say is true, he doesn't want the acclaim of those who do not really take him seriously.

Jesus does use publicity, but it is of an entirely different sort. It has credibility. He sends his disciples ahead of him into every town he intends to visit. Why? To prepare the way. Likewise, he is not afraid to instruct some whom he healed to stay and publish the news of the event locally instead of following him to other towns.

Both of these approaches have real credibility. They are rooted in real life. They are rooted in shared faith. The praise offered by the demons was empty and fake. It had no real content or meaning. It had no credibility.

The Scriptures also say that we should never praise ourselves, but that we should always leave that to others. In today's Gospel, Jesus heads off the possibility that his actions might be misconstrued as self-exalting. Here, with the messenger of lies, he goes to an extreme to insure the credibility of his ministry. He shows wisdom. With others, like the children at his triumphal entry into Jerusalem, he lets them praise him freely. It is a matter of intent and credibility. One is sincere. The other is still deceitful.

In all of this Jesus never exalts himself. He lets others call him the Messiah before he finally admits the truth of his nature and mission. He goes so far as to silence people in the beginning. Only towards the end of his mission did he admit the truth. It was this admission that would cost him his life.

Are we equally humble about our own mission? Do we show the same wisdom as Jesus in discerning true and superficial praise from so-called followers? Are we willing to pay the price for the truth of our mission when it is ultimately known to all? Finally, does our own praise of Jesus bear the marks of an innocent child or of a deceitful demon? In this regard, only children can enter God's kingdom. ☐

Respond to the Apostolic Faith
Mark 3:13-19 (2:Friday)

He then went up the mountain and summoned the men he himself had decided on, who came and joined him. v. 13

What kind of Christianity do we practice? Is it the apostolic faith of our fathers or some invention of a later era? What about our call today? Do we rely on the faith of the ancients alone, or do we have our own personal relationship with Jesus today, in the here and now?

Many forms of Christianity are novel indeed. Some cannot really be traced back more than a few tens, or hundreds of years, out of a history of almost two thousand years. That isn't very much. The concepts of "faith alone," or "Scripture alone" go back only four hundred years. Eschatological theories such as the pre-tribulation rapture go back only to the late 1800s, and the materialism of today's American Christianity is unique to our time. None of these were found in the early church. The issues are too many to deal with in today's short meditations. Suffice it to say that many of the so-called "Christian" teachings of today's modern American churches bear little resemblance to the apostolic faith that has come down to us from Jesus himself.

The early Christians did not follow the teachings of just any charismatic preacher who quoted Scriptures with his own interpretations. No, "they devoted themselves to the apostles' instruction" (Acts 2:42). Scripture alone was not enough. They needed the interpretation of Scripture from those who had been personally chosen by Christ himself. Jesus himself gave them their interpretation of Scripture

(Lk 24:27). Jesus commissioned them (Mt 28:18-20). Jesus gave them a unique gift of the Spirit to accomplish their task (Jn 20:22).

These apostles oversaw the succession of leadership in the churches they founded (Ti 1:5; Acts 14:23), so that in time the church formed "a building which rises on the foundation of the apostles and prophets, with Christ Jesus himself as the capstone" (Eph 2:20).

This apostolic tradition is not static. It is guided and animated by the Spirit. As Jesus says, "I have much more to tell you, but you cannot bear it now. When he comes, however, being the Spirit of truth, he will guide you to all truth" (Jn 16:12-13). As St. Paul says, "Guard the rich deposit of faith with the help of the Holy Spirit" (2 Tm 1:14).

The apostolic tradition of the church is rich indeed! Nowhere on earth will you find so much richness and so much balance. Nowhere will you find such a rich heritage of contemplative and mystical tradition. Nowhere on earth will you find so many different kinds of authentic renewal, all building up the body. Nowhere on earth will you find a theology as developed and so ready to dialogue with those of other faiths. Finally, nowhere on earth will you find another institution, secular or sacred, which has spoken out so consistently for basic human rights and prescribed tangible suggestions to help individuals, churches, and even governments to help bring the redemption of Jesus Christ to all peoples everywhere.

What about you? How are you personally entering into God's calling on your life? Jesus still calls you today. The Spirit still raises up individuals, movements, and communities in the church today to face the challenges of the world in which we live. If you want to radically follow Christ, you can. The heritage of the church is filled with men and women who dared to respond to that call. What about you? Do you have the courage to respond?   □

Family Feuds
Mark 3:20, 21 (2:Saturday)

His family ... came to take charge of him, saying, "He is out of his mind." v. 21

What do we do when our family doesn't understand our faith in Jesus? Jesus promises us that our family will not always understand or support our faith in him. He says to the apostles, "Brother will hand over brother to death, ... children will turn against parents and have them put to death. You will be hated by all on account of me. But whoever holds out till the end will escape death" (Mt 10:21, 22). Perhaps this is why he goes on to say, "Whoever loves father or mother, son or daughter, more than me is not worthy of me" (Mt 10:37). Luke uses even stronger language: "If anyone comes to me without turning his back on his father and mother, his wife and his children, his brothers and sisters, indeed his very self, he cannot be my follower" (Lk 14:26). Jesus demands an absolute and total commitment, a commitment even greater than that to our blood families. Jesus brings out the contrast between his family who said he was "out of his mind," and his real spiritual family, when he said, "Whoever does the will of God is brother and sister and mother to me" (Mk 3:35).

Does this mean we are not to love our family? Jesus does say, "You shall love your neighbor as yourself" (Mk 12:31). Surely our family qualifies as our "neighbor"? Paul says to Timothy that bishops and deacons are to "be good managers of their own children and their households" (1 Tm 3:4-12). He says "Wives should be submissive to their husbands as if to the Lord" and, "husbands, love your wives, as Christ loved the church" (Eph 5:22, 25). Surely, Jesus and the apostles desired that faith in Christ would fulfill the great commandment to love, and love would strengthen, rather than weaken, the family.

However, even this ideal had to come face to face with the reality of today's Gospel. Some believe and some do not. Even in the case of this happening between husband and wife, Paul writes: "If any brother has a wife who is an unbeliever but is willing to live with him, he must not divorce her. And if any woman has a husband who is an unbeliever but is willing to live with her, she must not divorce him. The unbelieving husband is consecrated by his believing wife; the unbelieving wife is consecrated by her believing husband. . . . If the unbeliever wishes to separate, however, let him do so. . . . God has called you to live in peace" (1 Cor 7:12-15). This is both idealistic and practical by the basic principle of love.

Does this mean that those who do not understand us are always unbelievers? The answer is "no." Today's Gospel indicates that Jesus' family possibly including even Mary, didn't fully understand him. At Cana, Jesus clearly shows that Mary does not really understand his mission: "Woman, how does this concern of yours involve me? My hour has not yet come." Yet she is still "full of grace" when she says, "Do whatever he tells you" (Jn 2:4, 5). No doubt, even the early church was filled with misunderstanding, despite the gift of the Spirit and the leadership of the apostles! Today's church is no different.

How do we relate to those who do not understand us? Do we love them or hate them? Even if they are our enemies, Jesus says, "Love your enemies" (Mt 5:44). Do we really "love" our family members who do not understand us? Can we still love them when they claim to be "Christian" and clearly aren't following Christ? Finally, can we or anyone, except Jesus, love them enough to be their Saviour? The one who can love us all the best is Jesus. If we love him more than anyone, we will come to really love everyone, especially our families. □

Discerning the Holy Spirit
Mark 3:22-30 (3:Monday)

He expels demons with the help of the prince of demons. . . . How can Satan expel Satan? Whoever blasphemes against the Holy Spirit will never be forgiven. vv. 22, 23, 29

We have already seen that Christians can only cast out demons in the name of Jesus, by the blood of Jesus, and with the integrity of a real life in Jesus. All else falls into the danger of magic and sorcery.

Jesus also says, "Many will plead with me, 'Lord, Lord, have we not prophesied in your name? Have we not exorcised demons by its power? . . . Then I will declare to them solemnly, 'I never knew you. Out of my sight you evildoers!' " (Mt 7:22, 23).

St. Paul says similarly, "If I have the gift of prophecy and, with full knowledge, comprehend all mysteries, if I have faith great enough to move mountains, but have not love, I am nothing" (1 Cor 13:2).

Apparently it is not enough to simply have a "powerful" ministry or to practice "power" evangelization. Our greatest "power" is love. The name of Jesus itself is powerless unless we have some understanding of the real meaning, the real person, the real God behind that name. The name is pronounced many ways in many languages, but Jesus himself can be understood by peoples of all races, cultures, and languages.

Today's Gospel reminds us that it is a dangerous thing, indeed, to speak against the ministry of a brother or sister, for is not the name of Jesus being preached? As David even said concerning Saul, "I would not harm the Lord's anointed" (1 Sm 26:23). St. Paul said during his trial before the Sanhedrin after he had insulted the high priest, "I did not know that he was the high priest. Indeed, Scripture has it, 'You shall not curse a prince of your people' " (Acts 23:5).

This can even be the "unforgiveable sin." Scripture says

that we can be assured of the forgiveness of all sin, if we only confess them (1 Jn 1:9) and repent (Lk 24:47). It is when we are so hardened that we cannot even repent that our sins become unforgiveable (Heb 6:4-6). Apparently, when we begin criticizing other ministries with a hard heart, we are dangerously close to this sin! Likewise, we should not let forgiveness of sin become an excuse to prolong sin. As Sirach says, "Of forgiveness be not overconfident, adding sin upon sin. Delay not your conversion to the Lord, . . ." (Sir 5:5-8).

Are we overly critical of other ministries or other expressions of Christian faiths? Does our lifestyle match our use of Jesus' name in ministry, prayer, and deliverance? Finally, are we so confident in forgiveness concerning things that we simply do not change? Do not delay. Change today! □

Spiritual and Blood Ties
Mark 3:31-35 (3:Tuesday)

Whoever does the will of God is brother and sister and mother to me. v. 35

Today's Gospel summarizes all of the teachings of the relationship between the Christian and his or her blood family. Yes, we have a blood family, but we also have a spiritual family. The two are both important. In fact, the two may overlap. Yet, according to the teachings of Jesus, the spiritual family takes precedent over the blood family.

Mark's Gospel contrasts the blood family and the spiritual family more than any other Gospel. Mark alone describes Jesus' blood family as saying of him, "He is out of his mind" (Mk 3:21). Mark alone is silent concerning Mary's participation in the life and ministry of Jesus and the early church. Mark clearly emphasizes the priority of the spiritual family over any earthly family.

Matthew includes the earthly family by including Mary's participation of faith in the birth of Christ, pointing out that

Jesus was to be found, "with Mary his mother" (Mt 1; 2). Luke also places an even sharper importance on the "infancy narratives" where Mary is called "full of grace," "highly favored," and "blessed" as "the servant of the Lord" (Lk 1; 2). He also places her with the early Christians in the upper room around Pentecost (Acts 1:14).

John alone includes Mary's presence at the beginning of Jesus' "ministry of miracles" at Cana where she says, "Do whatever he tells you" (Jn 2:1-12). John also includes Mary standing faithfully at the foot of the cross when all but John had fled. It was here that Jesus undeniably merged the blood family into the spiritual family through the faith of his mother and the "disciple whom he loved." He says to Mary, "Woman, there is your son," and to John, "There is your mother." The text concludes, "From that hour onward, the disciple took her into his care" (Jn 19:25-27).

From the example of Mary, we can clearly see that Jesus and the early church included her in the spiritual family through her faithful participation in his birth, his ministry, his passion, and the life of the early church around Pentecost. Clearly she must be included when Jesus says, "Whoever does the will of God is brother and sister and mother to me."

That the spiritual family of the church considered each other "brothers and sisters" and even admitted a spiritual fatherhood and motherhood for those who nurtured communities is self-evident.

Paul calls Timothy "my own true child in the faith" while bestowing on him the "grace, mercy, and peace" from "God the Father and Christ Jesus our Lord" (1 Tm 1:2). He depicts himself as a spiritual father, betrothing the church in Corinth, "in marriage to one husband presenting you as a chaste virgin to Christ" (2 Cor 11:2; see 2 Thes 2:13). He also talks of himself as a "mother" to the churches he founded (1 Cor 3:2). As to being true brothers and sisters, Paul says, "Your love must be sincere. . . . Love one another with the affection of brothers. Anticipate each other in showing respect" (Rom 12:9, 10). This is the language of a true spiritual family, a family of mutual love, full respect, and gentle intimacy. This spiritual family is real!

How do we view our brothers, sisters, and elders in Christ? Are they really brothers, sisters, fathers, and mothers to us, or are they simply nameless faces who fill the church pews—administrators and institutional teachers who preside at our altars and in our pulpits? What of our blood family? Is it more important than our spiritual family? Do we allow it to be incorporated into the family of faith, or is our Christianity an escape from the family responsibility that true Christian love brings? If we truly enter into the spiritual family in Christ, Jesus answers all these questions in one simple word: "love." □

The Power of Parables
Mark 4:1-20 (3:Wednesday)

He began to instruct them at great length, by the use of parables. v. 2

Christianity is not the fastest growing religion on earth. Islam is! Why? Islam is an oriental religion, born in the Middle East. Christianity was born in the Middle East but grew most markedly to the West to the Occidentals. Today, only a small part of the world is oriented towards the occidental mind of the West. Most of the world's population is oriented more towards oriental thinking.

What is the difference between the occidental mind of the West and the oriental mind of the East? One of the major differences is between logic and mystery. The occidental mind thinks in logic. The Eastern mind thinks in parables and mystery.

The use of the parable is an oriental tool that communicates profound truth by way of a simple story. It is able to communicate both logic and mystery at the same time.

It is interesting to note the way Jesus usually taught. He

taught by way of stories and parables! Rarely did he quote Scripture. For Jesus all creation became a vehicle for God's word. Yes, Jesus quoted Scripture to defeat the attacks of the devil (Mt 4:1-19) or to confound the teachers of the law (Mk 12:36), but when he taught the multitudes, he resorted to the mystery of parables.

In general, Christianity has not followed this example of Jesus. As Christianity spread West and grew up with the developing power of the empires of the West, it adapted the thinking and language of the West. Granted, the early church fathers used parables and analogies widely. By the time of the Protestant Reformation, however, this way of thinking was largely lost. Along with it we lost much of the mind and way of Jesus Christ.

Today, the powers of the West are declining. The oriental East is on the rise. The economic center of gravity has moved to the East. Where the economy goes, there will the next world empire appear. Likewise, Islam, a religion of the East, is spreading like wildfire. More and more, we westerners are having to face the fact that we are a minority people of this world, not long to be the major power of the world. Likewise, Christianity is not keeping up with the spread of Islam.

I propose that we go back to the mind of Christ in order to reach the mind of the world. This mind is oriental. Today's introduction into parables can hopefully introduce us back to our Middle Eastern roots of the Christian faith. □

Slow Cookin'
Mark 4:21-25 (3:Thursday)

Things are hidden only to be revealed at a later time . . . Listen carefully to what you hear. vv. 22, 24

Today's Gospel is an extension of the Jesus method of teaching with parables. How did Jesus learn these parables?

By observing nature and people and hearing God speak to him through the created world. This required silence. This required solitude. This required patience.

Today's world is in such a hurry! If we want to learn God's word we expect to be able to sit down and read it in a book, or hear it on a tape, or see it on a movie. While these things can be good, they do not teach you the richness of God's word.

Personally, I have learned many of the deeper truths of Jesus and the church by spending long hours alone in the woods or by observing the ordinary affairs of life. This is not something that just "happens." It requires a discipline that is intentional. I have learned many things of God by observing the flowing of a creek, the growing of a tree, the falling of snow and rain, as well as by observing people planting a garden or constructing a building, as well as falling in love. These are all ordinary things, but the Spirit has used them to speak extraordinary truths to the depths of my soul.

Jesus must have spent much time alone for such contemplation. Mark says, "He stayed in desert places; yet people kept coming to him from all sides," or, "he went off to a lonely place in the desert; there he was absorbed in prayer" (Mk 1:45, 35). Luke says, "He often retired to deserted places and prayed" (Lk 5:16). Likewise, from his stories, it is obvious that he knew the ordinary working of people very well. As his own townspeople observed in wonder, "Is this not the carpenter, the son of Mary?" (Mk 6:3).

No doubt, God's word comes to us in Scripture, but Scripture alone is not enough. We need the instruction of the Spirit (Jn 16:13; Mt 10:19, 20), but this is not enough either. Many have spoken nothing but their own feeling and intuition when they thought it was the Spirit. Many have spoken the Scriptures like a sword that kills and maims. We need to take the time in silence for deep contemplation. This is difficult for an "instant breakfast" and "fast food" culture such as ours. It requires time. It requires patience. Take time to listen and to observe. Be patient. Then you will hear and see the living word of God. Then you will know what "good news" we must proclaim.   □

Little Seeds Growing
Mark 4:26-34 (3:Friday)

The seed sprouts and grows without his knowing how it happens. v. 27

Is there any guaranteed plan for spiritual growth? There is not. Our communities and churches are filled with programs ... formation programs, evangelization programs, Scripture programs, call groups, support groups, sharing groups ... the list seems endless. Yet in the end it isn't any of these things in themselves that do God's work. God does!

There is only one absolute in today's parable: The seed grows from the soil. In order for the seed to grow it must first be buried and disappear. This involves the way of the cross.

As Jesus says, "Unless the grain of wheat falls to the ground and dies, it remains just a grain of wheat" (Jn 12:24). Likewise, St. Paul directly links the "fruit of the Spirit" with the cross; "The fruit of the Spirit is love, joy, peace, ... Those who belong to Christ Jesus have crucified their flesh with its passions and desires" (Gal 5:22-24).

This means dying to the logic of the world which demands that "big is better." Today's Gospel tells us: If you want to get bigger, get small. "It is the mustard seed which when planted in the soil is the smallest of the earth's seeds, yet once it is sown, springs up to become the largest of shrubs." As Jesus says concerning humility, "When you are invited [to a wedding party] ... go and sit in the lowest place, so that when your host approaches you he will say, 'My friend, come up higher' " (Lk 14:8-11). Concerning the importance of small things: "If you can trust a man in little things, you can also trust him in greater" (Lk 16:10).

This is why in our community, The Brothers and Sisters of

Charity, we believe you learn as much about spirituality by working a garden, or cleaning a building, or constructing a dwelling, as you do by prayer and study. Many come to us and want to be great contemplatives, or embark on great ministries. Unless they can dig in the dirt, or push a broom successfully, however, they will, more than likely, never be successful at any of these "greater" things of the kingdom. Likewise, unless they can love the life of the gospel in our community faithfully, they can never effectively share this way of our life with others. The "little things" are an absolutely vital part of spiritual formation.

A funny thing happens after a couple of years of this: You begin to change. You experience conversion. You start to grow up. The worldly characteristics that seemed so obvious at the beginning, slowly but surely disappear. Almost imperceptibly it just happens. After days, weeks, months, and years of faithfulness in small things, a great transformation takes place in a person's soul. They become more Christ-like!

Are you willing to disappear in order for Christ to appear fully in your life? Are you willing to do the little things in order for great things to truly happen in your soul? Have you ever considered doing this in the context of a community where the rubber of your life really hits the asphalt of other brothers and sisters? If you want great things "right now" you will probably fail. If you are patient in the small things, you will surely succeed! □

Resting with Jesus
Mark 4:35-41 (3:Saturday)

The waves were breaking over the boat and it began to ship water badly. v. 37

Today's Gospel has Jesus "leaving the crowd" in a boat. He had already preached to the crowd. Now it was time to rest. Notice, even in this "retreat," he was in a boat with others, and "other boats accompanied him." This was a solitude in the midst of his disciples.

How does he do it? "Jesus was in the stern through it all, sound asleep on a cushion." Jesus was able to rest in the midst of activity. He had learned the lesson of the psalms, "He pours his gifts on his beloved while they slumbered" (Ps 127:2), and was not afraid to seek rest in the Lord even in the midst of activity.

"It happened that a bad squall blew up. The waves were breaking over the boat and it began to ship water badly." Not only was Jesus seeking rest in the midst of the disciples' activity of travel, he was even sleeping in the midst of a dangerous storm! He was sleeping like a baby!

"Teacher, does it not bother you that we are going to drown?" This is no ordinary storm. It is a life-threatening catastrophe. Finally, they wake Jesus up! Why? Because they have faith in him to save them? Not entirely. There is not a little bit of annoyance in their voices, as if to say: He heals others, but allows us to drown! It is not really faith. It is desperation and accusation.

Jesus responds by calming the sea. Then he says to them, "Why are you so terrified? Why are you lacking in faith?" It is as if to say: Didn't you know that as long as I am with you, you will not perish? Why couldn't you just rest as I was doing?

Today's Gospel has two lessons. On the surface it teaches us that we can awaken Jesus in the midst of the storms of our life, and he will calm them. The Gospel says, "Who can this be that the wind and the sea obey him?"

However, the deeper lesson really has to do with resting in the Lord in the midst of the storm. Maintaining this rest and peace born of absolute trust in God the Father's sovereign will throughout all the "storms" of our world takes a far greater faith. Yes, God can, does, and will calm the storms if we ask him. How do we ask? In faith, or in desperation? In trust, or in accusation? If we really believe that Jesus is in our boat, we will never perish. It is up to him whether he wants to wake or sleep. □

Do We Love Familiar Demons?
Mark 5:1-20 (4:Monday)

They came to Gerasene territory . . . met by a man from the tombs who had an unclean spirit. vv. 1, 2

Today's Gospel teaches us much about the deliverance of evil spirits. As we have said before, this ministry is given in a special way to the apostles (Mt 10:8), and to the disciples (Lk 10:17-19), but is also given to all believers (Mk 16:17). It should never be undertaken lightly and should always be in union with church leadership. Many people have gotten into trouble by taking on a deliverance for which they were simply not prepared.

There are some important lessons in today's Gospel. First, the condition of the demoniac was extremely sad. "The man had taken refuge among the tombs; he could no longer be restrained even with a chain . . . Uninterruptedly night and day, amid the tombs and the hillsides, he screamed and gashed himself with stones." The demon was literally torturing this man, perhaps even killing him. This was no "demon hunt." The demon was obvious. It was also dangerous.

Secondly, the demon is "religious." It calls Jesus all the right names: "Son of God Most High." It even treats Jesus with respect, "I implore you in God's name, do not torture me." But its motives are not pure. St. James says, "The demons believe that and shudder" (Jas 2:19). It doesn't want to change. It isn't willing to repent. It only wants to acknowledge Jesus and remain the same. We, too, have grown accustomed to "comfortable" sins, "familiar" spirits. Are we willing to change?

Jesus not only rebukes the spirit. He asks the spirit its name, "Unclean spirit, come out of the man! What is your name?" It is important to identify evil or sin. It is not enough to vaguely seek God. As Jesus says, "Declare your sins to one another" (Jas 5:16). Whether in deliverance of a spirit, or in sin in general, it is important to identify the problem. An evil spirit must answer this question when asked with credibility in Jesus' name.

The spirit answers, "Legion is my name . . . There are hundreds of us." A person can be possessed or oppressed by many spirits. Furthermore, Jesus says after one has been cast out, if you do not immediately fill the human with the Spirit of God, many more spirits will come back to fill the empty space (Mt 12:43-45).

Notice that Jesus sends the unclean spirits to a certain place after he exorcises them. "He gave the word, and with it the unclean spirits came out and entered the swine. The herd then rushed into the sea and drowned." Of course, the symbolism of the swine as "unclean" cannot be overlooked, but the important thing is that Jesus didn't just cast out the demons. He sent them somewhere. We don't really understand the rules of the invisible sphere of good and bad spirits. We don't have the vaguest idea where to send them. But Jesus does! It is important to send the spirits to Jesus so that he can do with them whatever he wills.

Lastly, notice that this ministry isn't very popular. "Before long they were begging him to go away from their district." Why? Because the man had been delivered and restored to a normal and healthy life? I think not. It probably had more to do with the fact that Jesus had disrupted their normal business. He had destroyed their pigs! They were "swineherds." Pigs were their business. When Jesus casts out demons he changes things, not only in one person, but in a whole area. He changes personal and private sins. He also changes the corporate ones. This involves radical change.

Are we really ready to change? Are we willing to not only call Jesus Lord and to reverence his name, but to give up our own familiar spirits and comfortable sins? Are we really ready to enter into the now so faddish "deliverance" ministry, or should we not first learn the rules of the game before we play with fire? Are we willing to let Jesus change

our business, our whole way of life, in order to be his disciple
. . . to be delivered? Or conversely, are we willing to suffer
persecution and rejection so that others might be healed? □

Faith in the Face of Ridicule
Mark 5:21-43 (4:Tuesday)

Fear is useless. What is needed is trust. v. 36

Today's Gospel tells of two healings in the midst of one.
The main story is the healing of the synagogue official's
daughter. Within this story is the moving account of the
healing of the woman with the hemorrhage of twelve years.
One is a person of importance who approaches Jesus
confidently. The other is a woman too timid and tired to do
anything but touch the hem of his garment. Both have faith
and love. Both are healed by Jesus.

The synagogue official, named Jairus, "fell at his feet and
made this earnest appeal." The woman with the hemorrhage thought, "If I just touch his clothing . . . I will get well."

Jesus did not even intentionally touch the hemorrhaging
woman. She touched him. "Who touched my clothing?" He
said this even though a whole crowd was hemming him in,
no doubt touching him constantly. As Luke says, "The
whole crowd was trying to touch him because power went
out from him which cured all" (Lk 6:19). The account in
Mark says, "Jesus was conscious at once that healing power
had gone out from him." Apparently, there was a difference
between an ordinary touch of the crowd and the touch of
faith. As Jesus says, "Daughter, it is your faith that has cured
you."

With Jairus' daughter, by the time they had arrived, the
servants announced, "Your daughter is dead." How sad.
The salvation of one seems to have caused the loss of the
other. The original request seems to have been disregarded

for the interruption of another. But this is not the case. "Jesus disregarded the report." He goes on, "She is not dead, but asleep." The people at Jairus' household are astounded at Jesus' insistence on healing the girl even after she is reported to be dead. "At this they began to ridicule him." Sometimes healing takes faith in the face of apparent contradictory reports and persecution.

With both the woman and the daughter, Jesus' healing seemed to contradict nature and logic. The woman "had received treatment at the hands of doctors of every sort and had exhausted her savings in the process, yet she got no relief." Jairus' daughter was clearly reported to be dead. Jesus worked miracles that went beyond the natural science of medicine and the human understanding of the mind.

Are we willing to believe in the face of such natural conditions and reports? Are we willing to seek Jesus' healing even when we are ridiculed? Today's Gospel encourages us to keep believing even when we seem to be getting no natural results. Then we will see supernatural miracles! □

Perceiving Our Own Prophets
Mark 6:1-6 (4:Wednesday)

No prophet is without honor except in his native place. v. 4

How do we treat the prophets in our midst? If they are able to "prophesy" with power in other places, why can they not do so at home?

Suffice it to say that those around Jesus could not see past the natural to the supernatural. They could only say, "Is this not the carpenter, the son of Mary, a brother of James and Joses and Judas and Simon? Are not his sisters our neighbors here?" They were unable to understand what Simon Peter, the other fisherman, understood when Jesus said to him, "Come after me; I will make you fishers of men" (Mk 1:17). Jesus was still a carpenter, but now he was building the house of God!

Notice that Jesus still did some pretty amazing things there. "He began to teach in the synagogue in a way that kept his large audience amazed." Apparently, he taught differently than anything they had heard before. "Where did he get all this? What kind of wisdom is he endowed with?" As is said earlier, "The people were spellbound by his teaching because he taught with authority, and not like the scribes" (Mk 1:22).

He also worked some miracles in Nazareth. Granted, the text may read, "He could work no miracle there . . . so much did their lack of faith distress him." But it also includes, "apart from curing a few who were sick, by laying hands on them." He must have worked some miracles in Nazareth or they would not have said, "How is it that such miraculous deeds are accomplished at his hands?"

The problem was not that Jesus didn't preach, teach, and heal at Nazareth. He did! The problem was the people's response to such a powerful ministry. They saw the supernatural, but they immediately fell back to the natural. The gift was given, but they gave it back. They wouldn't accept it. Because of this, Jesus went away. "He made the rounds of the neighboring villages instead, and spent his time teaching." Their time had come and they missed it.

How do we receive God's visitation in our midst? It may come by a sovereign act of God independent of a human vessel, or it may come through a person we have known for years. Do we really see and receive the supernatural, or do we fall back to the natural? Many powerful ministers have friends that receive them only as "good people." While this is important, it can cause family and friends to miss the truly supernatural phenomenon God is doing right in their midst.

Such phenomenon don't make us holy. They make us responsible. What have we done with God's prophets in our midst today? □

The Unique American Heresy
Mark 6:7-13 (4:Thursday)

He instructed them to take nothing on the journey. v. 8

Today's Gospel is the "rule of life" for the itinerate ministry of Christian history. Our history is filled with the wandering preachers and prophets raised up by the Spirit in the church with a zeal for God and God alone.

How different are the modern ministries of the West. The successful evangelist is often epitomized by an extravagant lifestyle out of reach for most of those to whom they preach. It propagates the error of Western materialism and the heresy of American Christianity. What is this error? What is this heresy?—that if you have much wealth, you are truly successful, that if God is really with you, you will be rich.

Of course, this flies in the face of real Christianity. Jesus never preached this, nor did the apostles. Paul never preached it. Augustine or Chrysostom never preached it. Benedict or Basil never preached it. Gregory or Bernard, Francis or Dominic, John of the Cross or Theresa of Avila, Luther, Calvin, or Ignatius of Loyola, John Wesley, or George Fox never preached it. It is only the evangelists of this era in America who began to make a theology out of materialism.

Still, we need to be careful not to become fanatical or overly literal in our understanding of gospel poverty. Today's Gospel differs from other accounts. Mark says to take "a walking stick" and "to wear sandals." Matthew and Luke say not to take these things (Mt 10; Lk 9; 10). What does this seeming contradiction mean?

Using a more literal interpretation, it would indicate that

Jesus sent them out many times and at different times of the year. In the Middle East you cannot go barefoot in the summer. The heat dries up all things green and soft, leaving only brown thistles along the path. These rip the unprotected foot to shreds. Likewise, the excessive heat makes the use of a walking stick a near necessity for long walks under the blazing Middle Eastern sun. All turns green and soft with the winter rains. Neither walking staff or sandals are absolutely necessary. It rarely gets really cold.

This means that Jesus adapted his poverty to the circumstances. It was not always the same externally. It did, however, remain the same internally. What is this internal constant?

Matthew's version gives us a hint to the answer: "The gift you have received, give as a gift." If you are burdened by many possessions, you lose your freedom. If you are no longer free, then you cannot give away anything freely. This is true both emotionally and economically.

Today's Gospel encourages us to be truly detached and free from the world in order to more effectively bring salvation to the world. Is our ministry really free? Do the "tools" of our infrastructures free our ministries or make them slaves to maintenance? Jesus wants our ministries to be free. He wants us to rediscover the ministry mode of the saints. Then will America's "heresy" be corrected. ☐

To Risk Hearing a Living Word
Mark 6:14-29 (4:Friday)

Herod feared John ... When he heard him speak he was very much disturbed; yet he felt the attraction of his words. v. 20

So it is with God's Word. It calls us to repentance. It calls us to change. While this is always a change for the better, this change is not always easy. It can be upsetting. It can be a challenge. It can cut to the core of our secular ideas.

As Hebrews says, "God's word is living and effective, sharper than any two-edged sword. It penetrates and divides soul and spirit, joints and marrow; it judges the reflections and thoughts of the heart" (Heb 4:12).

Yet God's Word is also irresistible and sure. As the psalmist says, "Your Word, O LORD, endures forever; it is firm as the heavens" (Ps 119:89). Regardless of a person's final response, the Word never goes out without some effect. It stirs up response. As Isaiah says, "It shall not return to me void, but shall do my will, achieving the end for which I sent it" (Is 55:11). God's Word is not passive. It activates response in the depths of the soul.

But the "Word" heard by Herod was not just the written Word of Scripture. It was the living Word of a Spirit-inspired prophet. It was not "safe" as dead letters on a page. It was fully alive and powerfully unleashed in a living, breathing, servant of God.

Paul recognized that the Word of God came through his preaching. To the Thessalonians, he writes, "in receiving his message from us you took it, not as the word of men, but as it truly is, the word of God at work within you who believe" (1 Thes 2:13). Similarly, he says to the Galatians, "you took me to yourselves as an angel of God, even as if I had been Christ Jesus!" (Gal 4:14).

What is it that John said that made Herod so uncomfortable? First, the essence of John's message was repentance . . . change. "Reform your lives! The reign of God is at hand," (Mt 3:2) was at the heart of all he said. He went on to some challenging applications (Lk 3:1-18). More specifically, he publicly challenged Herod for marrying his brother's wife, Herodias, in violation of the law. As today's Gospel says, "Herod was the one who had ordered John arrested, chained, and imprisoned on account of Herodias, the wife of his brother Philip, who he married. That was because John told Herod, 'It is not right for you to live with your brother's wife.'" Eventually, this cost John his head at the plotting of Herodias and cost Herod his honor, and perhaps even his soul!

John's message was the living Word of God. It was specific, personal, and challenging. It was irresistible and effective. It made Herod uncomfortable by a call to personal repentance that had tangible and dramatic effects on his personal domestic way of life. Furthermore, it cost him his life!

Are we willing to hear such living words through our brothers and sisters in the church? Are we really willing to change even the "comfortable" sins which affect our whole domestic way of life? Lastly, are we willing to proclaim this living Word of God to others even when it costs us our security, our freedom, and perhaps even our life itself? □

Time with Jesus
Mark 6:30-34 (4:Saturday)

". . . Come by yourselves to an out-of-the-way place and rest a little. . . ." v. 31

The disciples had just returned from active ministry. They had been commissioned with "authority over unclean spirits . . . they went off, preaching the need of repentance. They expelled many demons, anointed the sick with oil, and worked many cures." They also traveled in radical poverty. "He instructed them to take nothing on the journey but a walking stick—no food, no traveling bag, not a coin in the purses in their belts" (Mk 6:7-13). Luke's Gospel in particular, tells us of the great success of the similar ministry of the seventy-two (Lk 10:17), and the rejoicing of Jesus at their success (verse 21). But now it is time for rest. It is time for solitude.

You cannot put in a day's work unless you have first had a

good night's sleep. Similarly, you cannot have good active ministry unless you also take the time for spiritual rest and revitalization through prayer. You cannot give what you do not possess. If you want relationship with Jesus, you need good, quality time to build that relationship just with him. After that, then you can share this relationship with others. It is like fueling a fire. If you don't take the time to put a little wood on the fire, the fire will eventually go out. Likewise, if we don't take time for prayer and rest in solitude, our apostolic activity will eventually become ineffective. We will work intently in the name of Jesus, but never really accomplish his will.

Some people are very afraid of this. They are convinced that if they do not do the job, it simply won't get done. Needless to say, there is always a job to do. If you try to do them all, you begin a sure course to eventual self-destruction. This is egotism. It is the classical "Messiah complex." Yes, God wants us to work sacrificially, and each of us has a unique gift to offer the church and the world, but no one is that indispensable. As we say here in our community: Everyone is important; no one is indispensable.

Furthermore, some people are afraid of solitude and rest because it will bring them face-to-face with God and themselves. In solitude and rest there is no activity or work to hide behind. It is just you and God. This is scary if you have never faced this stark reality. As we also say: If you are afraid of solitude, beware of community.

But the converse if also true: If you are afraid of community, beware of solitude. Solitude and rest can also become a selfish escape from the real demands and responsibilities of life in the church and the world. Sometimes the greatest way to get close to Jesus is to work side-by-side with him in the church. As we also see in today's Gospel, the crowds follow Jesus into solitude. He doesn't turn them away. It becomes another opportunity to work a miracle.

The greatest way is really neither a life of constant solitude nor the way of constant apostolic action. The greatest way is the way of Christ himself. It is neither the contemplative life nor the apostolic life, it is the evangelical life. We simply follow Jesus in solitude and in action and find in the balance a life based squarely on the good news, the Gospel of Jesus. □

"Jesus on the Spot"
Mark 6:53-56 (5:Monday)

Wherever he put in an appearance . . . they laid the sick in the market places and begged him to let them touch just the tassel of his cloak. All who touched him got well. v. 56

Where do we make an appearance today? It is easy to heal people in Jesus' name when you are ministering at a healing service. It is expected! But what about in the "market place"?

Most of us spend the greater portion of our time in the market place. We spend very little time in church and even less time at a charismatic healing service. Jesus was much the same. Yes, he went to the synagogues when it was appropriate. But he spent most of his week and most of his day in the normal environment of life. He was "in the market place."

This did not keep Jesus from healing. His healing ministry was not limited to a healing service or the times when all were watching. He was open to heal at all times. He was ready on the spot!

We too are called to be "Jesus on the spot." We are called to bring the healing of Jesus Christ whenever we put in "an appearance." If someone is in need of prayer, we should pray! If it is possible, pray right then and there. Pray on the spot! Don't wait! Tomorrow may never come. Pray now! Ask for healing now. If we are "Jesus on the spot," then Jesus will heal "on the spot." If we wait, he might simply use someone else or not heal at all.

Jesus teaches us to let our whole life shine when he says, "your light must shine before men so that they may see goodness in your acts and give praise to your heavenly Father" (Mt 5:16). Of prayer, St. Paul says, "never cease praying, render constant thanks" (1 Thes 5:17, 18). To Timothy he says, "In every place the men shall offer prayers with blameless hands held aloft" (1 Tm 2:8). We are to pray in the market place as well as in the church, not for ourselves, but for the sake of others.

How are we to pray? Certainly with the essential basics of the Lord's Prayer (Mt 6:9-15). But also with an expectant faith. "If you are ready to believe that you will receive whatever you ask for in prayer, it shall be done for you" (Mk 11:24). Likewise, pray with an accepting faith. Not my will, but, "let it be as you would have it" (Mt 26:36-46). So we are to accept and expect. Then we will see miracles. Then we will avoid the sin of presumption.

Are we really ready to be "Jesus on the spot"? Are we ready to pray and offer healing in any form whenever we put in an appearance? Do we really expect a miracle when we pray? Are we really humble enough to accept God's answer after we do? All of these questions must be answered if we are to heal as Jesus healed. If we find the right answers in our life, then like Jesus, they will begin bringing the sick to us, not only at the healing service but even in the market place. We will learn the secret of being "Jesus on the spot." □

Vain Tradition Can Lead to Hellish Living
Mark 7:1-13 (5:Tuesday)

You disregard God's commandment and cling to what is human tradition. v. 8

I once sat next to an orthodox Jew on a plane from London to Los Angeles. This man was extremely obese, clothed with layer upon layer of traditional orthodox clothing, and sweating profusely. Consequently, the odor was almost intolerable.

Upon being seated, which took quite some time, he began to pray from his prayer book in traditional orthodox style. When he was through reciting his prayers, he pulled out some food, performed all the prescribed sprinklings and washings, ate, and then prayed again. When these prayers were over, he ate again . . . being scrupulous about every detail. This cycle went on, over and over, for the entire trip . . . some twelve hours! Consequently, instead of eating the normal number of meals with the other passengers, he ate almost every hour: close to ten meals, complete with prayers, sprinklings, and washings. Now I understand why he was so obese!

What had gone wrong? This man had tried to center his life on God. But he got sidetracked into all the various prayers of orthodox Jewry. Perhaps because he was overly conscientious, he soon became scrupulous about these prayers and rituals. Because so much of his own daily routine centered on dietary ritual, he ate all the time! What had begun as a good idea for orthodox Jews became a bad idea. What began as a celebration of life with God began to actually kill this poor man.

This is an extreme example of what Jesus is talking about in today's Gospel. Tradition is a fact. It is also inevitable. This includes the sacred and the secular. Within the sacred this includes divine tradition and human tradition. In and of themselves these traditions are not bad if they lead you to God. However, it is an irony of all religions that the very traditions designed to lead us to God often degenerate into taking us away from God.

This happens when conscientiousness degenerates into scrupulosity. Soon we try to fulfill all the traditions, divine and human in origin, placing equal importance to them all. Then we simply run out of time. Our life is so filled with tradition, there is no more time left to really observe the commandments of God. Religion becomes idolatry, and scrupulosity with ourselves becomes judgment of others. In the name of God, we soon find ourselves living in our own private hell.

This process is not limited to the faith of the orthodox

Jews. No! We can see it clearly in many of our Christian churches. Liturgy, ritual, and even the Scriptures and the sacraments can actually take us away from Jesus if we approach them too scrupulously, or worship the gift instead of the Giver, the instrument of grace rather than Grace itself. We are interested in one thing only: a personal love relationship with Jesus Christ. Any doctrine, any sacrament, or any church structure that does not center entirely on bringing us into this personal love relationship with Jesus as a united people is pointless and vain.

I can say confidently that these things in the Catholic Christian faith can lead us to Jesus. Usually, the problem is not the doctrine, the sacrament, or the church structure. Usually, the problem is with us. The problem is the attitude in which we approach these things and share them with others.

Today look into your own heart. Is your attitude right? Is your religion centered on Jesus and Jesus alone? If it is not we might be guilty of practicing "vain traditions"! □

Purge Your Heart
Mark 7:14-23 (5:Wednesday)

Nothing that enters a man from outside can make him impure; that which comes out of him, and only that, constitutes impurity. v. 15

Jesus is interested in the heart. It is on the heart that the New Covenant is written. It is on the heart that Paul's letters are primarily written (2 Cor 3:2, 3). Without the heart no religious act of the flesh or intellectual pursuit of the mind is complete. The heart is absolutely essential in real Christianity.

Perhaps this is why Paul contrasts love to all other religious acts in 1 Corinthians 13. He says that none of the charismatic gifts of tongues, prophecy, knowledge, or faith, mean anything at all without love. Likewise, the work of peace and justice by giving all your possessions to the poor or your body to be burned are meaningless without a real heart of love.

This is also his basis for his teaching on faith. He says, "a man is not justified by legal observance but by faith in Jesus Christ" (Gal 2:16). He goes on to say that this is a "faith, which expresses itself through love" (Gal 5:6).

He is very clear that this applies to imposing the rite of circumcision on Gentile Christians. He is so adamant that he says, "if you have yourselves circumcised, Christ will be of no use to you! . . . Would that those who are troubling you might go the whole way, and castrate themselves!" (Gal 5:1-12). No doubt, Paul is battling the tendency to return to an externalism that is not first based on internal faith and love.

Jesus, too, is capable of some very crude analogies concerning this religious tendency. He says in today's Gospel, "Nothing that enters a man from outside can make him impure. It does not penetrate his being but enters his stomach only and passes into the latrine." Why is he so adamant and crude? Because the real issues are immediate and grave! "What emerges from within man, that and nothing else is what makes him impure. Wicked designs come from the deep recesses of the heart—acts of fornication, theft, murder, adulterous conduct, greed, maliciousness, deceit, sensuality, envy, blasphemy, arrogance, an obtuse spirit. All these evils come from within and render man impure." It is easy to engage in all these sins which bring death to ourselves and others while fulfilling the externals of religious observance with seeming piety. Jesus is more interested in the heart. So were his first followers.

What about us? Do we grow as upset when a person living a saintly life fails to satisfy an external religious observance as when a person fulfilling external piety falls into secret sin? Perhaps we are sometimes that person.

Today, Jesus calls us back to the heart. He calls us to keep the importance of religious ritual in its proper place. It is never as important as the heart. Ritual can change, but the heart must remain pure if we are to really please God. □

Rich Masters and Humble Dogs
Mark 7:24-30 (5:Thursday)

Even the dogs under the table eat the family's leavings. v. 28

Today we come upon the issue that forced the early church to rethink its whole approach to the external demands of the Jewish religious law: the conversion of the Gentiles to Christianity. On one level it was rather easy for a Jewish Christian to simply look to the heart of the law while obediently fulfilling its external demands with the new meaning of the Spirit. It was even easy to deal with a few Gentile converts according to the mandate of the law. When these Gentile converts began to constitute first a substantial number and then even a majority of the Christians, clearly a change was in order. The Gospels of the early church tell their stories of Jesus in light of this pressing early church issue.

This part of Mark's Gospel is clearly trying to deal with the pressing issue of the Gentiles. Yesterday we considered the real importance of the dietary law. Today we see Jesus deal directly with a Gentile.

This is significant. Usually Jesus is presented as the complete Jew. He is clear that the Jews are the chosen people. He even hesitates to minister to those who are not Jews. He only hints that a time will later come when the Gentiles will be directly included. But today Jesus deals directly with a Gentile.

In today's story Jesus again reaffirms the position of the Jews: "It is not right to take the food of the children and throw it to the dogs." These "dogs" were the Gentiles as normally described by the orthodox Jew. As Jesus said even to the woman from the Samaritan origin, "after all, salvation is from the Jews" (Jn 4:22).

How does the "dog" of today's Gospel win the healing response of Jesus? By demanding her rights as a recipient of the foretold New Covenant? By forcing Jesus into this universal ministry? No! By humility! She said, "Please, Lord . . . even the dogs under the table eat the family's leavings."

We also have "Gentiles" and "Jews" in modern Christianity. We could call the "Jews" those who can trace a historical, apostolic succession directly back to Christ. The "Gentiles" are outside this apostolic company. As Paul said of the Jews, "Theirs were the adoption, the glory, the covenants, the law-giving, the worship, and the promises." Likewise, we could rightly say: ours are the apostolic succession, the apostolic tradition, the Scriptures, and the sacraments.

We had best be careful! Are we really humble in the midst of our differences today? Do we really value the legitimate gifts of today's "Jews"? Are we "Jews" really open to bringing the richness of apostolic tradition to those outside its boundaries? Such mutual openness and humility is absolutely mandatory if we are to be fully united again in Christ. □

Gossipers Kill
Mark 7:31-37 (5:Friday)

The more he ordered them not to, the more they proclaimed it. v. 36

There is a principle at work in modern office communications: If you want to make sure that the whole office finds out about a decision, call a confidential meeting behind closed doors! If you want a policy followed in a half-hearted, lazy way by your employees, announce it publicly as common knowledge. What does this say about human nature?

Unfortunately, it says that the tendency of modern society is toward sin. Gossip is usually communicated with more zeal and interest than open and honest dialogue. As St. Paul said so long ago: "There is no just man, not even one; all have taken the wrong course, . . . not one of them acts uprightly, no, not one. Their throats are open tombs; they use their tongue to deceive; The venom of asps lies behind their lips. Their mouths are full of curses and bitterness" (Rom 3:10-14). So it was, and so it is, that the tendency to gossip is related inherently to the universal bondage of sin.

That this sin is truly destructive, Paul continues: "Swiftly run their feet to shed blood; ruin and misery strew their course. The path of peace is unknown to them; the fear of God is not before their eyes" (Rom 3:15-18). As Dietrich Bonhoeffer once said, the gossiper is the same as a murderer. It is only the device that is different. One uses the tongue. The other resorts to an external tool. But the effect is the same: death, murder, destruction.

We have found that this is one of the more difficult problems in building intentional Christian community in America. It is so problematic that we take special pains to fight it. We fight it with the clear teaching of the gospel. If you have something negative or critical to say, say it directly to the person. If they will not listen, then bring in another person directly involved with the issue. If they still don't listen, then bring in leadership. If you go outside of this procedure, then you are guilty of gossip. Of course, you may discuss anything with a spiritual director or confessor. But even discussion among friends quickly degenerates into gossip in the name of "concern" or "counsel." Gossip is a grave and serious moral offense. It kills. It is verbal murder.

Do we get more excited about a secret story than we do about an open truth? Why? Do we tend to gossip? Have we tried to verbalize this sin under the guise of conversation among friends? Let us simply be obedient today. When Jesus tells us not to say anything, let us simply be silent! □

God Pities Us
Mark 8:1-10 (5:Saturday)

My heart is moved with pity for the crowd. v. 2

Why did Jesus work miracles? Was it simply to manifest God's power? Was it only to evoke the people to have faith in him? I think not. Jesus worked miracles out of love. Yes, these other aspects were definitely involved, but Jesus never worked a miracle that did not have a good effect on those who were the recipient of his power. His miracles came from love.

This is brought out very clearly in the Acts of the Apostles' account of his whole life and miracles. This account says very simply, "I take it you know what had been reported ... about Jesus of Nazareth, ... of the way God anointed him with the Holy Spirit and power. He went about doing good works and healing all who were in the grip of the devil, and God was with him" (Acts 10:37-38). His works were good. His miracles overflowed from love.

By its definition, "good" must overflow from itself to another. Likewise, "love" must not only overflow out of oneself to another, but it produce another from the love union of the two. This is why God is said to be both loving and good. Within his trinitarian form he could be truly selfless even when nothing else existed. He is One and Three. He is self-sufficient in transcendent Oneness, and selfless in goodness and love in Trinity. This is part of the great mystery of the Trinity.

However, God's love and goodness is much more than just a theological mystery. It is tangible and clear. God did not have to create, but he did. He chose to out of love. Furthermore, he has freely chosen to care for us and redeem us in our weakness and our sin. He could simply forget us. That would be just. After all, humankind has sinned. We have pretty well ruined planet earth and all life on it. Still, God continues to reach out in his superabundant goodness and love to try and help us.

That is the message of the Gospel today. Jesus works miracles out of love. The crowd is groping for an answer. They have taken the risk to follow Jesus. No, they didn't plan well. They ran out of food. But they at least followed. They tried. Because of this Jesus will work a great miracle for them. He will feed them in abundance. They have risked. He does not let them down.

What about us? Will we take the risk? Will we follow the way of Jesus even against all logic? Will we trust in the miracle of love? If we will, we will also have all our needs met, with much more love from God. He will not let us down. □

Jesus Mournfully Sighed
Mark 8:11-13 (6:Monday)

With a sigh from the depths of his spirit he said, "Why does this age seek a sign? I assure you, no such sign will be given it." **v. 12**

Jesus gets exasperated with his listeners. How reassuring to know that even Jesus got frustrated when he was not being understood. This exasperation and frustration is not necessarily a sin. In fact, it is the lot of most leaders in the church, if not with all of us at one point or another.

But this "deep sigh" is not mere impatience. Impatience is contrary to love. "Love is patient" (1 Cor 13:4), says St. Paul. Impatience is a superficial response. Jesus' response was a sigh from the depths of his heart. It was deep. It was honest. It was much more than the knee jerk reaction of impatience. Therefore, it could be validly expressed in love.

Today's Gospel speaks specifically of Jesus' frustration with the religious leaders of his day. Tomorrow hits a little closer to home with his frustration with his own disciples. Today he speaks, not to those closest to him, but to those of the organized and institutional religion.

However, their immediate distance from him in experience is no excuse. They were the ones who were supposed to be studied in the Scriptures and the things of God. They were the ones who were freed from the burdens of ordinary, daily living in order to devote themselves fully to the things of God and ministry to God's people. Yet they are the ones who perhaps misunderstand Jesus the most. They are the ones who ultimately reject him and put him to death. Despite their study of God and their ordination from God, they still do not understand the will of God.

It is no different today. Sometimes, the ones whom religious society has set aside for the full and unhindered service of God are the very ones who continually misunderstand and actively block the will of God. This has nothing to do with the validity of their ordination or state of life. It is a simple irony of human nature. St. Francis said eight hundred years ago that those who devote too much time to sacred study and are put in places of leadership and honor are the very ones in most danger of losing their docility to the real will of God. It is no different today.

Do we sometimes grow frustrated with our religious leaders? As religious leaders, do we sometimes miss the will of God despite our constant efforts to focus on God? Today, Jesus sighs from the depths of his spirit. He wants so badly for all to understand, but we do not. This is a normal condition in our abnormal world. It is a fact of life in a fallen world. We, too, must learn to deal with it like Jesus did. □

Christianity Is Counter Culture
Mark 8:14-21 (6:Tuesday)

Do you still not see or comprehend? Are your minds completely blinded? v. 17

Today Jesus' deep response of frustration shifts from the Pharisees to his own disciples. Jesus had just concluded warning them about the "yeast of the Pharisees and the yeast of Herod," which had frustrated and exasperated him in yesterday's Gospel. But they did not understand! This leads him to a similar exasperation with them.

Jesus' words to his own disciples in this vein are many and they are strong. He says on various occasions, "What little sense you have," or "How slow you are to believe...!" (Lk 24:25). Even in the famous Last Discourse of John's Gospel, Jesus is still saying to the apostle Philip, "After I have been with you all this time, you still do not know me?" (Jn 14:9). Jesus was amazed that his own apostles and disciples did not really understand him despite their continued closeness to him. He was not afraid to express this to them.

I must say that as founder and leader of our community, I can certainly relate to these frustrations. Sometimes, despite repeated teaching and instruction on certain points, many people simply do not comprehend. Worse yet, if they do comprehend, they simply choose to disobey. Furthermore, despite being given repeated opportunities to change through repentance and the support of counseling, some simply refuse. Then to my further amazement, they cannot understand why they cannot remain in the community.

The reason for some of these specific problems in Christian community is our American culture. Americans are an individualistic, materialistic, and promiscuous people. Community emphasizes obedience, simple living, and chaste relationships. It has been seriously questioned whether or not Christian community really works in a culture such as ours. We want what we want when we want it. We "did it my way." Real Christian community runs counter to these trends. It is counter culture.

America is in desperate trouble. God has repeatedly warned us through our own contemporary, prophetic voices that we must change, or our nation and civilization will fall. We have not heeded his voice. Communities such as ours do what they can to respond to God's call, but even we find it difficult to overcome our inbred, cultural sin. This is frustrating to us. It is frustrating to our leaders. It is frustrating to God.

Still no cultural sin is beyond the grace of God. We can change if we wish. The question is: do we really want to change? The answer to that question will decide the future of our world as we know it. It will decide salvation.

Are we afraid to express our frustrations? Furthermore, what are we willing to do with them? Do we act constructively on these frustrations, or do we just criticize others? If we express frustration, then we must do our best to provide a solution to the problem in Christ. We must become a part of the solution rather than a part of the problem. Even if we fail in the effort, God and others will know that at least we tried. □

Progress with Patience
Mark 8:22-26 (6:Wednesday)

A second time Jesus laid hands on his eyes, and he saw perfectly.
v. 25

Even Jesus had to try more than once in healing the blind man at Bethsaida! In a sense you could say that Jesus' own example gives credence to the old saying, "If at first you don't succeed, try, try again." No doubt, there are many areas in our own Christian life where this is necessary.

The Christian life is a process. Perfection doesn't happen overnight. Total perfection doesn't happen at all, but a substantial mastery over various problem areas of our life is possible. All of this takes daily work and patience. You don't broad jump into victory and healing. You usually go one step at a time.

Jesus tells us to take up our cross daily. St. Paul tells us of the struggle within his flesh and his spirit so that he still often did the things his spirit didn't want to do. St. John tells us of the continual process of confession, repentance, and forgiveness. These things don't happen once and for all. They happen over and over all through our Christian life.

Ministry to others is also a process. Just as we must be ministered to repeatedly through many steps, so must we minister to others through many repeated steps. This is the essence of today's Gospel. Jesus healed the blind man of Bethsaida through steps. It didn't happen all at once. It needed to be repeated.

In a sense, this also happens with ministry in general. Jesus says that if they don't receive you in one town, shake the dust from your sandals and move on the the next. Again, this involves repetition. It is repetitive for those who minister. It is also repetitive for the given region in which the various towns are located. If you don't reach the region through one town, try another. If you don't reach a state through one region, try another. And if you don't reach a nation through one state, try another state. This all involves repetition. It also involves patience and perseverance.

Are we willing to "try and try again" in our whole Christian life? Losing a battle does not mean you have lost the war. Today's Gospel teaches us that even Jesus used a process to heal the blind man at Bethsaida. It wasn't instantaneous. We should not be discouraged if sometimes we must do the same. □

My Ways Are Not Your Ways
Mark 8:27-33 (6:Thursday)

"You are the Messiah!"... Peter then took him aside and began to remonstrate with him. At this he ... reprimanded Peter: "Get out of my sight, you satan! You are not judging by God's standards but by man's." vv. 18, 32-33

Peter is the man of impetuosity and contradiction. Whatever he does, he does all the way! Therefore, he is the first to proclaim Jesus as the Messiah. But he turns right around and becomes an instrument of satan himself by trying to keep Jesus from going to the cross, which is the primary purpose for which Jesus came into the world! He can be "the rock." He can also be like shifting sand.

Notice how Peter moves from the rock upon which Jesus will build his church, to an instrument of Satan. He begins to judge by human standards. One minute he is proclaiming Jesus as Messiah by a wisdom that can only come from divine revelation. As Matthew's Gospel has it: "Blest are you, Simon son of John! No mere man has revealed this to you, but my heavenly Father" (Mt 16:17). The next minute he has returned to human logic alone and again becomes an instrument of Jesus' subtle enemy.

By human logic alone, Peter's objection seemed loving and good: don't go to Jerusalem if those who want to kill you are in Jerusalem. Simple logic, right? But not God's wisdom.

As St. Paul says, "The message of the cross is complete absurdity to those who are headed for ruin, . . . It is not a wisdom of this age, . . . Yet God has revealed this wisdom to us through the Spirit. . . . The natural man does not accept what is taught by the Spirit of God" (1 Cor 1:18; 2:7, 10, 14). As the Old Testament had already said, "For my thoughts are not your thoughts, nor are your ways my ways" (Is 55:8).

We are really not unlike Peter. At one moment we are filled with great spiritual insights and virtue. The next moment we have reverted to our old ways. Yes, we have been given the Spirit in a way Peter had not yet received, but we still experience the struggle between the Spirit and the flesh, the old and the new.

It is usually not very apparent. It may seem quite logical. It could be a day-in and day-out matter of running a family, a community, a business, or a ministry within the church. It may be a matter of guiding the church. It may seem harmless enough and even go unnoticed by others, but God knows. He knows when we operate in the Spirit or in the flesh. He knows when we seek wisdom, or when we simply use human logic alone.

God wants to use our mind, but we must open it to him through prayer and meditation on God's word. Then will we be given the mind of Christ. Then will we receive the Spirit fully and grow beyond a life of contradiction to a life of harmony and mystical paradox. Peter eventually did this after the giving of the Spirit at Pentecost and a long life of spiritual growth within the church. If Peter did it, we can too! □

The Cross Requires Change
Mark 8:34; 9:1 (6:Friday)

If a man wishes to come after me, he must deny his very self, take up his cross, and follow in my steps. v. 34

Today Jesus takes us beyond the wisdom of his cross, to our cross. He begins to make clear the wisdom from the Spirit that so eluded Peter in yesterday's Gospel. He also gives some bottom line requirements for living the life of a disciple.

Jesus begins with the first step of response: change. It has been said in modern times that Jesus accepts us just as we are. As the hymn goes, "Just as I am, I come." There is truth to this, but left there, this concept is really quite wrong.

On one level, Jesus meets us just where we are. He calls us to himself no matter how sinful we might be. He says, "Come to me, all you who are weary and find life burdensome" (Mt 11:28), and "The healthy do not need a doctor; sick people do" (Lk 5:31). Jesus meets us in our sickness, no matter how bad our condition.

Jesus also calls us to change. Repentance is the essence of the first sermon Jesus ever preached. To the rich young ruler, he gave instructions to change by giving his possessions to the poor *before* he could actually follow Jesus. Today's Gospel demands action in order to fully respond to grace.

Once we do this hard, cold, objective change of lifestyle and begin to seriously follow Christ, then the mystical graces follow. After we tangibly take up our cross, then we begin to see its mystical wisdom. Then we really see the wealth in poverty, the freedom of the yoke of obedience, the fulfillment of chaste human love or union with God alone through the vow of chastity. Until you actually embrace the cross by the action of a changed life, these concepts remain only words. After you have acted on these words, then these concepts become a mystical reality, reflecting the wisdom of God.

Are we really willing to change our way of life to follow Christ? Are we willing to act in order to receive God's grace? Are we willing to risk the actions of a fool to be truly docile to the wisdom of God? These are the questions of today's Gospel. The answers will determine whether or not you have moved from mere human logic to the real wisdom of God: the message of the cross! □

Transfiguration Requires Discipline
Mark 9:2-13 (6:Saturday)

Jesus took Peter, James, and John off by themselves with him and led them up a high mountain. He was transfigured before their eyes. v. 2

How often we want mystical graces or charismatic gifts. However, are we willing to be transfigured according to the way of Jesus Christ? This way is challenging. It takes work and patience to play by Jesus' rules. Today's Gospel gives us solid guidelines to lead us to Christ-like transfiguration.

First, it takes discipline. Jesus was constantly going into solitude to pray. To do this meant staying up into the night and rising up earlier in the morning. Today, it also meant expending the time and energy to climb the Mount of Transfiguration. For those who have ever walked up Mount Tabor in the Holy Land, you know this climb is not altogether easy! It will not be easy for us to provide the time and space for solitary prayer away from the crowds of daily life, but it must be done if we are to share in the transfiguration of Christ.

Second, it requires community. It cannot be done alone. Jesus goes into solitude with others. Ironic as it sounds, you cannot maintain a lasting discipline of solitude and silence without the support of other like-minded brothers and sisters. Without their support the average Christian will eventually succumb to the hectic and busy pressures of modern living. Likewise, without first meeting the love responsibility of committed relationships in Christ, solitude becomes the ultimate cop-out. Christian solitude is never an escape from reality. If confronts the greatest reality: God! Likewise, it must confront the realities of life in God's church and God's world.

Third, it is done in real communion with the saints. Jesus was in communion with Moses and Elijah, two saints from the ancient past who represented the law and the prophets. Likewise, we must be in full communion with the apostles, prophets, and saints of the past if we are to live our Christian life radically in the present and build to the future. Scripture says, "You form a building which rises on the foundation of the apostles and prophets, with Christ Jesus himself as the capstone" (Eph 2:20).

Lastly, all of this must give glory to Jesus and Jesus alone. Impetuous Peter wanted to erect monuments or shrines to the saints. God said not to do so, but only to listen to Jesus. Furthermore, glorious as this communion of saints was, when it was over, they could not see anyone but Jesus. All of our mystical experiences of any kind must lead us only to Jesus. If they lead us anywhere else, they are not really from God.

Are we willing to pay the price of discipline in order to open the way for the gift of grace? Is our solitude an escape from community, or is it done in union with the church? Are we in full communion with the saints of old, or do we limit this communion to those now living? Lastly, does our mystical experience glorify Jesus or someone else? All must be for Jesus only, then will our transfiguration truly be "like Christ" or Christian. □

Part II

The Lenten Season

Turn Back to God
Matthew 6:1-6, 16-18 (Ash Wednesday)

Be on guard against performing religious acts for people to see. **v. 1**

What is the essence of the good news of Jesus Christ? Repentance. Penance. Conversion. It isn't bad news. It is good news. It changes us. It converts us from death to life, sorrow to joy, unhappiness to happiness. Repentance is the most essential message of the gospel of Jesus Christ.

Ash Wednesday is the beginning of the season of Lent, a season of repentance. It isn't something to be glum about. It is good news. It is a season to turn to God. It is like a person who is walking towards the drop-off of a high cliff. Once they discover that they are headed towards certain injury and death, it just makes good common sense to turn around, to convert, to do penance. So it is with Lent. It just makes good sense to turn back to God. It saves your life.

Still there is more to conversion than the logic of self-preservation. There is love, a matter of the heart.

When you have offended someone you love, it causes your heart to hurt. It is not just a matter of logical reconciliation in order to keep the relationship in full operation. It is a matter of sorrow and contrition, because it is a matter of love.

The same is true in Lenten conversion. We turn to God with a twinge of sorrow in our heart because we have offended God's heart by our sin. This is a matter of the heart, a matter of love, a matter of personal relationship with God. If there is no sorrow, then perhaps there is really no love in your relationship with God.

There is also some pain because of obedience to God's truth. Yes, God's truth sets us free, but following God's truth is not always easy. It is difficult to break off a bad habit or relationship that hurts us in the long run. It seems to hurt more in the short term, but in the long run this obedience brings greater comfort because it is in accord with God's truth that comes from a greater love.

Penance also brings some pain because of the cross. The cross is the greatest expression of God's love . . . that Jesus would die for us that we might live. This is sacrifice. Without sacrifice there is really no love. Our Lenten sacrifices are sometimes actual opportunities to sacrifice out of love for God and people. Sometimes they are symbolic—like fasting and prayer—but they are all precious to God's heart if done out of love for him.

Are we really ready to sacrifice this Lenten season? Are we ready to come back to truth? Do we really love, or is religion just ritual and legal observance to us? Are we really ready to turn back to the heart of God?   □

Selling Your Soul
Luke 9:22-25 (Thursday)

What profit does he show who gains the whole world and destroys himself in the process? v. 25

I can remember the classic movie "Man For All Seasons," about the martyrdom of St. Thomas More in England. During the trial St. Thomas is betrayed by his young and ambitious friend Richard, who has been promised to be made a leader in Wales if he will lie about Thomas. After the lying betrayal Thomas looks straight at the young ambitious Richard and says, "Christ says it is sad to lose your soul for the world. But Richard, to lose your soul for Wales?" The comical content caused the whole court to laugh at Richard, even though his lying betrayal had enabled them to convict Thomas More. The moral: It is the little things of the world that cause us to lose our soul.

We are not that different from Richard. We too are ambitious. Be it secular or religious, most of us are concerned about climbing the ladder of success. We may not lie like

Richard did or even commit some overt sin, but most of us place success over God at some point in our life. Sometimes we even commit the subtle idolotry of placing success for God over God himself. This is the most devious and most treacherous of deceptions.

Like Richard, our "Wales" is usually quite small when seen in perspective. Even from the worldly perspective the possessions we "must" have in our homes do not even measure up to the finer things of the truly wealthy. Yet we are willing to place them above God in order to obtain them. Our positions of power are usually quite low on the totem pole when seen against the truly powerful of this world. Yet we are willing to ignore the Most Powerful in order to snatch up our little empire.

Of course, from the eternal perspective, even for the world's rich and powerful, the things of this world are rarely worth the loss of your soul. A brief look into the personal lives of the rich and powerful reveals that most of them have never achieved real and lasting happiness. Their stories are filled with emptiness and pain.

What are the "Wales" of our lives? Where have we denied Jesus Christ for the trifles of this world? What little thing of this passing world is really worth the loss of our souls? Even with the religious, where has our work or prayer for God subtly become a substitute for God himself? Today's Gospel encourages us to seek God and God alone.   □

Fasting for Freedom and Peace
Matthew 9:14-15 (Friday)

Then they will fast. v. 15

Jesus gives us only three teachings on fasting. Today is one of those. Another is found in the Sermon on the Mount where he tells us not to fast as the hypocrites but to groom our hair and wash our faces so as to hide our fasting from onlookers. The third is found in Mark's Gospel where after the transfiguration Jesus says certain demons only come out through fasting and prayer.

Today's Gospel presents a paradox: the already and the not yet. On one level we can say that the bridegroom is always with us. Jesus promised us that he is with us always, even to the end of the age. Furthermore, the Spirit is now with us always, unlike with the psalmist of Psalm 51 who had to pray that the Holy Spirit be not taken away from him because of his sin. The Spirit can be stifled. It needs to be stirred up; but in the New Testament the Spirit is never taken away from the believer.

This means that, in one sense, the bridegroom is never gone, so we need never fast. But in another sense Jesus sometimes seems far away indeed. He has ascended to the Father and will come back at the end of the age. Sometimes it seems that, despite the gift of the Spirit, we are still quite alone. This is when Jesus says we will fast.

Jesus doesn't say "if" we fast. He says "when" we fast. He gives fasting a new meaning. He takes it back to a fasting from the heart rather than a mere external exercise. He never says, however, that the New Testament believer will not fast.

He also returns it to the original meaning of Isaiah the prophet. Here it is an external sign and symbol of internal conversion and self-sacrifice. It is to help set the prisoner free and to restore peace. What good is it to fast when our lifestyle is not really about these greater sacrifices and services? If we do fast, our general lifestyle must also be setting captives free.

Do our lifestyles speak of a "fast" in order to set others free? Do we always feel like Jesus is present, or does he sometimes seem far away? Is our fasting to be a glum experience in religiosity, or is it a joyfully fought battle with the assurance of victory? □

Step By Step
Luke 5:22-32 (Saturday)

"Follow me." Leaving everything behind, Levi stood up and became his follower. vv. 27-28

Are we willing to literally stand up from our job and follow Jesus? Levi was a tax collector. He was a businessman. Financially, he would have been quite well-to-do according to the average business wages of Jesus' day. No doubt, Levi understood all too well the almost stifling reality of business infrastructure and responsibility. He might have been successful, but this success comes with a price. Jesus is offering to pay the debt and set him free.

What was this new life to which Jesus called him? It is the life of Matthew 10. It is a life of strict itinerant wandering from place to place with no money, no possessions, and no attachments. This new freedom would allow the apostles to spread the gospel throughout the known world after Pentecost. At the very least it is the life of Acts 2 and 4 where all believers shared all things in common ownership; or 2 Corinthians 8 where real equality between the rich and the poor was volunteered from one's private possessions. Regardless of the particulars, this life was a radical change from the materialism of the typical tax collector in the time of Christ.

Before we get all excited about walking out of our business commitments to "hit the road for Jesus," we had better read on. The next scene finds Jesus at Levi's house eating and drinking with a somewhat undesirable crowd, his former friends. He may have "left everything," but here he is in the midst of his old way of life with Christ! This means that Levi might well have decided to leave everything and follow Jesus, but he had to proceed one step at a time. He could not do the "broad jump" for Christ without falling flat in the sand.

What about us? Are we willing to take the "leap of faith" with Levi and stand up from our established business to follow Jesus? Are we willing to let Jesus set us free? Only he can do it, but it will require a change—radical change of our whole way of life with which we are comfortable and in which we find our security. At the same time are we patient enough to proceed one step at a time? Are we willing to invite Jesus into the real concrete situations of our present life and let him walk with us out of bondage? We must be willing to do either if we are going to let Jesus walk us out at his pace. The challenge of radical gospel living is real, but it can overwhelm us if we do not start right where we are, taking one step at a time. Take the first step. After a while we will discover that we can travel a great distance. □

Great and Small Mercies
Matthew 25:31-46 (1:Monday)

"As often as you neglected to do it to one of these least ones, you neglected to do it to me." These will go off to eternal punishment and the just to eternal life. v. 45

This is the strongest account of judgment in the words of Christ. It is also one of the strongest accounts of mercy. Therefore, there is a definite link between showing mercy to people and being judged by God.

Jesus' words start with the little things. Whatever we do to the least of these his little ones, we do unto him. This means thinking small: looking to the ones immediately close to us, our family and friends, the people we work with. This isn't "big stuff." It starts right at home.

This doesn't mean we shouldn't think about more global dimensions of mercy. Most of the world goes to bed hungry. Most are not properly cared for medically. Most are not properly educated or trained vocationally. The minority of the world consumes the majority of the world's resources. We bear a responsibility to do something about this global imbalance.

This is what supporting a relief and development ministry is all about. This very gospel is the inspiration of Mercy Corps International, the agency of which Pat Boone and I are honorary chairpersons. It is also the inspiration behind many other Christian relief and development agencies. Hopefully, we all regularly support at least one.

There is a third category for mercy. Our own domestic poor. Granted, they are still the middle class of the world, and the reasons for poverty in the midst of an affluent society are complex, but we cannot simply ignore the problem if we still claim to be Christian. The street people, the plight of the American farmer, or the migrant worker, not to mention the medical problems such as the AID's epidemic are all areas for mercy ministry. St. Vincent de Paul, Meals on Wheels, food banks, and street shelters are just a few places to begin. If nothing exists in your area, start something new or work with an existing network. Do something!

All of us need to do something in each of these areas. Giving to the bigger mercy ministries without being merciful in your own immediate circle of family, community, and friends can become a cop out. So can never giving to the bigger global programs by saying we are already doing something at home. God has given us so much. How can we not share it with others?   □

How to Pray
Matthew 6:7-15 (1:Tuesday)

In your prayer do not rattle on like the pagans. . . . This is how you are to pray: "Our Father . . ." vv. 7, 9

It is a sad irony that often we defeat the very purpose of the Lord's Prayer in praying it. It is not so much the prayer itself that is wrong. The prayer is given by Christ! It is the way we pray that is wrong.

In the average parish I am astounded by the way the Lord's Prayer is said. It is prayed as if we are running a race! Many times I find myself actually out of breath by trying to keep up the pace. The same could be said of the way many good devotional prayers are recited. This practice clearly defies the intent of Jesus Christ himself.

I am reminded of a good experience with Bernard Cardinal Law, Archbishop of Boston. Other evangelists and I were gathered for a meeting on evangelization in the archdiocese. At the close of one session we began to pray the Lord's Prayer. Cardinal Law stopped us midway and encouraged us to slow down a little so that the prayer not be prayed vainly. I dare say it was one of the most evangelistic programs discussed all day.

The Lord's Prayer itself is the most perfect prayer on earth, yet it is one of the simplest. When asked how to pray, Jesus did not teach some complicated prayer method or technique. He simply gave us this short prayer and urged us to pray with sincerity.

The prayer itself covers most of the essentials of spirituality: That God is to be hallowed as the transcendent one, yet without losing the loving intimacy of a Father; That his kingdom is to come on earth as in heaven; That we are dependent on God for even the bare essentials of daily existence; That forgiveness is essential in relationships, both human and divine; And finally that God is sovereign over good and evil and is able to deliver us all from evil if we really desire it. It is so simple, yet so complete.

Do we really cherish the richness of this prayer when we pray it? The early Christians prayed this prayer three times a day; morning, noon, and night. For them it was sacred. Most of us pray it less than that. Do we take it as seriously? □

Demanding Wonders
Luke 11:29-32 (1:Wednesday)

This is an evil age. It seeks a sign. But no sign will be given it except the sign of Jonah. v. 29

Although Jesus works many signs and wonders, he is always clear that signs and wonders in and of themselves are never enough. He admits that without signs and wonders people won't believe.

The Old Testament is filled with admonitions to remember the signs and wonders of old. It also is unashamed to petition the Lord to work new signs and wonders. In the New Testament the followers of Jesus are assured that signs and wonders will follow their ministry. Yet Jesus always seems a bit perturbed that it takes signs and wonders to stir up the people's faith. He seems more comfortable working them simply to help out people who are in need.

Regarding faith, he seems more impressed by those who believe without seeing miracles or signs. He tells Thomas that the real "blessed" are those who believe without seeing. Likewise, Paul says that real faith is that which continues without seeing. The dependence on signs and wonders is definitely demanding to "see" before we believe.

This is true in many charismatic circles today. The phenomenon of "resting in the Spirit" has come to be seen as the "sign" of the Spirit's presence. Without it, some think the Spirit isn't really moving. In our itinerate ministry we often find a person going from prayer team to team until they "go under" the Spirit. Granted, with some people repeated prayer is necessary and useful, but clearly this approach is an abuse of a legitimate gift today and a traditionally evident gift among the saints. When we see this, we simply tell people to go sit down and receive what has already been given.

Of course, there are many other signs people seek. Tongues, healings, and prophecies are common among charismatics. The miracle of the sun is common among those with a strong Marian devotion when they visit Medjugorje. Mass conversions at a revival are common among evangelicals. All of these can be from God. All of these can, and have been, abused.

Do we seek signs and wonders, or do we seek God? If it takes repeated signs and wonders to keep our faith alive, then maybe our faith is not really in God. Maybe we just like excitement. □

Expect and Accept
Matthew 7:7-12 (1:Thursday)

Ask, and you will receive. Seek, and you will find. Knock, and it will be opened to you. v. 7

The word for today is action! There are three active words in today's Gospel: ask, seek, and knock. Asking is a matter of petition. It is also a matter of poverty. To ask of another is to admit that the other has a power that you do not have. It also is to be a matter of selfless love, for love is never centered on self. It is also a matter of humility, for humility admits its own powerlessness in certain areas.

This is not to say that there should not be a confidence in asking. Jesus says we must believe that what we ask for in prayer will be done, or it will not be granted. He likens this attitude to the attitude of a child towards its father. The child knows the father will always look out for the child's highest good in granting or denying the request. To be a child is to be humble, yet confident. We expect our parents to help us and humbly accept what they give us. We expect, then we accept. The same is true of asking something of our Father God. How sad that this analogy often breaks down in modern society where family relationships between parent and child are often torn with abuse, violence, and abandonment. Re-establishing this parent/child relationship with God is a good place to start in healing our broken relationships on earth.

Asking of God comes down to two concepts: expect and accept. We must expect a miracle when we ask of God, or we will rarely ever see God's miracles in our prayer life. After we have confidently asked God to answer our prayers, really believing that he will do so, then we must accept the way God answers our prayer. We must believe that he is truly our loving Father who is interested in the highest good in every situation.

Do we understand this balance in asking things of God? Do we really expect a miracle when we pray? Do we then accept how God's miracles occur? Do we really see God as a loving Father? All of these things affect our actively asking God in prayer. □

Letting Go, Letting God
Matthew 5:20-26 (1:Friday)

Everyone who grows angry with his brother shall be liable to judgment. v. 22

Anger is a major problem today. Oh, it is not obvious. It is no longer socially acceptable to break out in a duel with someone who has hurt you; nor is it acceptable to break out in arguments or tantrums in the professional world. No! We tend to surpress our anger nowadays, but it is still there.

Today anger comes out in less obvious ways. We control other people so we can hurt others "professionally." We enter into habitual relationships that are destructive to ourselves and others. Frequently, the problem is not even with the person or thing with which we have the destructive relationship. It is with someone from our past, or it is with ourselves. We end up projecting this anger with ourselves and others onto every relationship in our life. It destroys everything we try. It haunts us like a ghost. This kind of anger is not a good thing.

Usually anger starts small. It also starts early. Someone in our past hurts us in some way. It could be a mother or father, a brother or sister, or teacher, or minister. Usually they do not even know they have offended us. They just do something, and we either take it wrong or blow it out of proportion. Sometimes it is a major wrong, but we still don't handle it in a way that will set us free from the haunting curse of anger.

How should we handle anger? First, admit that you have it. Admit someone has made you angry. This is much healthier than pretending it isn't there. Pretending only causes it to fester like a boil. Sooner or later it will explode. When it does, it will be more destructive than ever.

Then confess to another person. Next try to resolve your differences. If there is anything you can do to make amends for any wrong, do it. Make repayment. Ask forgiveness. If you don't feel you have done anything wrong, at least ask forgiveness for any unnecessary hurt you may have caused without knowing it.

Finally, let your anger go. Forgive the person you are angry with regardless of how they respond. Give it to God and let God take care of the situation. Remember that he loves you more than you love yourself. This is also true of all other people. God can handle the justice of a matter much better than we can. Once you have done all you can do, let go of the situation and let God handle it. Then you will be free.

Are you angry today? Have you been angry for a long time? Maybe for years? Maybe most of your life? Be reconciled to God and others as soon as possible.   □

Love Your Enemies
Matthew 5:43-48 (1:Saturday)

Love your enemies, pray for your persecutors. v. 44

In facing the issues of today's world it is easy to develop an "us and them" attitude. It is easy to see the people on the other side of the Christian position as the "big, bad, and ugly." Sometimes we begin to actually hate the people who so radically oppose us Christians. This attitude itself is not in line with the teaching of Jesus Christ in today's Gospel.

This attitude is difficult to overcome. Many people involved in peace and social justice issues find it hard to love their enemy. This is because they have seen the sometimes devilish destruction enemies have wrought. The atrocity of an aborted fetus discarded in a trash barrel behind an American abortion clinic is an example. The sight of brutally beaten Palestinian children or tear-gased Christian clergy in Israel are others. Likewise, the sight of starving people living in a ghetto slum built on a trash heap in many Third World countries, while we of the West continue in blatant materialism, is enough to make you a little bitter, to say the least. I myself have had to fight to overcome bitterness towards the oppressors of this world.

Jesus tells us we must love even our enemy, the oppressor. This does not mean that we are not to continue to stand up for legitimate issues of justice, nor does it mean that we are not to actually hate sin. It does mean that we must love the sinner.

I am reminded of a man who once was almost obsessed in his persecution of Christians. He used to drag them out of their homes and meeting places and bring them to trial. He actually participated in the killing of a Christian saint and martyr. The martyr's name was St. Stephen. The persecutor's name was Saul of Tarsus. If you recall, Saul went on to become a martyr and a saint himself, the great St. Paul. How could he have gotten to be St. Paul if Christians didn't somehow bring themselves to love him?

Do we love our enemies? Have we grown angry and bitter towards the people on the other side of the issues we face? If we have, then we are no longer really Christians. We must come back to Christ if our issues are not to degenerate into a mere peace-and-social-justice gospel. Jesus says "love your enemy." □

Judge Righteously
Luke 6:36-38 (2:Monday)

Do not judge, and you will not be judged. v. 37

We are a people stuck in the middle. God wants to remove our blinders. He wants us to see from the far left to the far right. He wants to take us from narrow vision to an expanded view.

Our culture often exists in the middle regarding judgment and mercy. In an attempt not to judge, we have become overly permissive, yet our hearts are still clouded with judgment, bitterness, and anger. Our courts let criminals go free, while the abused are put on trial. They do this in an attempt "not to judge unfairly." Likewise, our churches are sometimes afraid to speak out against harmful teachings on faith and morality, but the orthodox are ridiculed and persecuted. This is not what Jesus had in mind. It does harm to people. Jesus came to help people. He wants us to understand mercy and judgment.

First, we must understand that judgment is simply a part of life. To deny it is to be unreal. Jesus might command us not to judge, but he also commands us to judge offending brothers and sisters and to treat them as "a tax collector or a sinner." This means ignore them. Have nothing to do with them. This is heavy judgment indeed! Paul also says not to judge those outside the church. Yet he follows Jesus' teaching in excommunicating the man who was having illicit sexual relations, so that the later forgiveness would be meaningful and real.

In the early church the bishops also had to make similar judgments. If an unrepentant murderer, or thief, or adulterer came forward and expected to be received into full communion, they would be denied full fellowship and reception of the sacraments. If they really repented and changed, they would be forgiven and received again.

This forgiveness was meaningful and rich indeed. It is like

a cup left outside in the rain. God's rain of forgiveness falls all the time, but some cups have been left upside down. They cannot collect the rain. Through repentance the cup is turned right side up so it can collect a full measure of God's forgiveness and grace. We too must repent before we can experience God's forgiveness.

Judgment cannot be made without mercy. The words for mercy and compassion mean not just to sympathize, but to empathize with other people. It means to really get inside their skin. We cannot properly judge anyone or any situation until we get inside the situations and motives of the people involved.

Lastly, we must let go of the seemingly endless judgments of mind and heart that go on inside us daily. Our life is a constant stream of judgments of other people's actions. This sucks us down into a cesspool of negativity that makes righteous judgment impossible.

Do we really judge righteously? Are we afraid to confront difficult issues? Are we really ready to get inside of other people, or are we too selfish to make the effort? Are we ready to let go of our inner judgments and let God take control? God wants to take us from our narrow vision to an expanded view. He wants us to let go of our incomplete human judgments. □

Mind the Mustard Seed
Matthew 23:1-12 (2:Tuesday)

The scribes and the Pharisees have succeeded Moses as teachers; therefore, do everything . . . they tell you. But do not follow their example. vv. 2-3

Who are the scribes and Pharisees? Who are the "religious"? They are us, you and me.

In today's world the followers of Jesus no longer face an older institutional religion that constitutes a majority. Christianity has become a traditional world religion. It is the majority in many places of the world.

This is both a blessing and a curse. It means that God has blessed us so that we have grown and prospered. This was prophesied by Christ's parable of the mustard seed. We did start out the smallest seed and have become one of the largest shrubs.

Jesus' parables also teach us that this is a problem. The wheat and the weeds do grow up together in the kingdom of God on earth. We cannot rightly separate the weeds and the wheat at this point in growth without accidentally pulling out the wheat as well. Only the angels of God can do this at the end of the age. This means that both true believers and false believers must grow together in the church for a season. This means the scribes and Pharisees must grow up in the church alongside of the true disciples of Jesus.

Sometimes the scribes and Pharisees are not "them." Sometimes "they" are "us." Sometimes the struggle between the scribe and Pharisee and the true disciple of Jesus Christ goes on right within our own heart. Sometimes we are the scribe and Pharisee without even knowing it!

Do we really see this as a grace? Are we willing to change when we see it within ourself?   □

Humility
Matthew 20:17-28 (2:Wednesday)

The Mother of Zebedee's sons came up to him . . . "Promise me that these sons of mine will sit, one at your right hand and the other at your left, in your kingdom." vv. 20-21

A brother with gifts in singing once came to our community. I invited him to sing harmonies with me in concert. At one concert his mother approached me and asked me in a confrontational way why her son was not singing more of the solos. I was a bit taken back by her question and her tone. Sometime later I decided to resume singing in concert by myself. Upon being told of my decision, this same brother told me I would lose a good part of my audience, because they actually came to hear him sing. Obviously, something had gone wrong.

Now I will tell you of a sister who came to our community. She had been a religious sister for a number of years, trained and experienced in parish ministry and religious community, but she only desired to be a servant. She was happy cleaning toilets and sweeping floors. She only sought to be obedient to the other sisters, even though they were less experienced, not as highly trained, and less exemplary in their way of life.

This made the other sisters in our community quite nervous and threatened them greatly, so they asked the serving sister to leave. Today this other sister is now in charge of all the sisters in our community. She is also now my wife as we both pioneer the married monastic way of life in today's church.

These two stories represent two aspects of today's Gospel. The first shows a mother and a son who were much like Zebedee's sons and their mother at the beginning of their time with Jesus. The second portrays a person who went through the journey with Christ to arrive with the apostles at a more humble and mature period of their lives. Both show servants of Christ, but at two different periods in their walk with the Lord, at two different levels of maturity.

Jesus wants to use our gifts and talents, but he usually uses them in a way totally unsuspected by us. If we keep our talents alive by trying to figure out and negotiate their use by God, God will never have the opportunity to fully resurrect them. If we let them totally die, then and only then will they be fully resurrected and used mightily by God.

Where are we today? Have we come to sing a solo or to wash a toilet? Have we come to serve or to be served? Anyone who comes to serve Christ with their own agenda of even religious career building cannot serve him at all. They serve themselves. Anyone who comes willing to do the most menial and insignificant of tasks will be lifted up by Christ and called great in the kingdom of God. □

Gleaning from the Saints
Luke 16:19-31 (2:Thursday)

If they do not listen to Moses and the prophets, they will not be convinced even if one should rise from the dead. v. 31

The communion of saints is a wonderful reality. Do we really appreciate this magnificent gift? Does it affect our lives?

The more I grow as a Catholic Christian, the more I am amazed that other followers of Christ do not accept the ancient teaching of the communion of saints. It seems that Christian life without the experience of the communion of saints as described in the Book of Hebrews and the Revelation, would be like a black and white picture compared to full color, or doing spiritual warfare with only part of our spiritual weapons and armor.

In our community, we believe that we are building on the foundation of the apostles and the prophets with Christ Jesus as the cornerstone. This building did not stop with the apostles. It has continued uninterrupted through almost two thousand years of history. We want to build squarely on top of those who have radically followed Christ before us. We do not want to simply imitate them, but we do want to be deeply inspired by them as we continue to build up higher into space and time where no one has gone before.

Still, St. Francis says it is not enough to simply read about the saints, or to be able to quote them. We must be saints. We must live in our own day and time with the same radical resolve to be a disciple of Christ that inspired the saints of old.

In today's Gospel Jesus says that even the experience of the communion of saints does no good if a person isn't open to being obedient to what has already been given in Scripture. If we aren't really open to the basics of the gospel, the communion of saints will do little good. There are many people who can quote the lives of the saints fluently, but cannot tell you much about inspired Scripture. This lacks the basic foundation. Conversely, there are many who are at a loss to tell you much about how this has been fleshed out in the lives of the real people and saints who constitute our living Christian history. This can be artificial and legalistic. Today's Gospel warns us about the first extreme.

Do the lives of the saints really inspire us to live the gospel? Does our knowledge of the lives of the saints focus or distract us from living the basics of the gospel? Conversely, do we know the written account of the gospel, but know little about how it has actually been lived in space and time? We need to know both and then apply them in practical ways.   □

The Punch of Parables
Matthew 21:33-43, 45-46 (2:Friday)

When the chief priests and the Pharisees heard these parables, they realized he was speaking about them.... they sought to arrest him, . . . vv. 45-46

Parables are a funny way to communicate. Because they are in a story form, they always seem very artistic or beautiful. Precisely because they are parables, they usually have a moral or religious meaning that can, indeed, pack a punch. This punch can be quite uncomfortable if you are the one being hit.

Today's parable seems to be about a property owner, some greedy tenant farmers, the messengers, and the son of the property owner. The parable is really about God the Father, the religious leaders of Israel, and the Son of God.

Needless to say, it indicted the religious leaders for not accepting Jesus and made them quite angry.

King David was also told a story of injustice by the prophet Nathan. At the end of the story Nathan asks the king what should be done with the guilty party. The king recommended a just, but harsh, sentence . . . death! At this point Nathan reveals to King David that the story is about him. David immediately repents before God and Nathan and is given a less harsh penalty. He is allowed to live (2 Sm 12:1-13).

There are two ways we can respond when convicted by a religious parable. We can resist and become angry like the religious leaders of Jesus' day. We can humble ourselves and repent like King David who was a man after God's own heart even after his sin. The choice is ours.

Parables speak to us on many levels. That is their beauty. They are so simple, yet almost inexcusable in their application. The same is true of today's parable. It is true of the ministry of Jesus, but it is also true of the Christian ministry in general.

Whom do we identify with in today's story? Are we the tenant farmers or the messengers, or the son of the property owner? God wants his people to be converted from greed to the way of justice. Let this parable speak to you about your own life. Then be converted!   □

The Challenge of Penance
Luke 15:1-3, 11-32 (2:Saturday)

We had to celebrate and rejoice! This brother of yours was dead, and has come back to life. He was lost, and is found. v. 32

Penance is an opportunity for joy. It is not a sober affair for downcast spirits. It is not a task accomplished by imposed rules against one's will. It is the turning from sin to righteousness as an act of the free will. Yes, it may take effort and even the guidance of a confessor, director, or superior, who might impose some helpful disciplinary measure. Granted, our own will may not seem immediately pliable to the will of God in these matters. However, at least a general desire to turn back to God in the church or a community of the church must be embraced as an act of a person's own free will.

Sin brings death. Righteousness brings life. Sin promises happiness and fulfillment. But it is a lie. Only the righteousness given as a gift in Jesus really brings freedom and abundant life. This takes more discipline. It takes patience, perseverance, and faith in times of darkness and struggle, but its rewards are longer-lasting. This effort has a big pay-off.

What about the other two characters in today's parable? There is the father and the faithful son. The son who never left is more like many of us. We never leave the faith or the church. We never engage in dissolute living. We never fall into the pit so that we have nowhere to go but up. The message to us is one of challenge and comfort: "You are with me always, and everything I have is yours." This is reassuring, but contains a challenge: "But we had to celebrate and rejoice, . . ." This confronts our jealousy when another person not seemingly as deserving as us gets a lot of recognition in the church for their "conversion."

The father also presents a challenge. He does not stay safely at home and wait for his wayward son to come home. No. When he sees him coming toward home, even at a distance, he runs out to meet him where he is and walks with him the rest of the way. It was more work, but the joy was greater.

Do we meet others where they are when they show the first signs of a desire to turn back to God, or do our churches expect them to travel most of the way themselves? Are we jealous when others receive much attention for their conversion to Christ, when our life of consistent faith is apparently taken for granted? Lastly, do we turn back to God, the church, or our community when we see that life outside really does lead to death? These are the challenges of today's Gospel. ☐

Discomfort with Authorities
Luke 4:24-30 (3:Monday)

No prophet gains acceptance in his native place. v. 24

How do we respond to the authority of those we know? Is it easier to accept authority from those far away or close?

Jesus was rejected in his home town, but he was accepted in other towns. As he became more known by all, he was eventually rejected by all. Why?

Somehow it is easier to hear a hard teaching from an outsider. No doubt, many a religious superior have shaken their heads in amazement when their community accepts a teaching or prophetic word given by a guest retreatmaster, when they have rejected that same word given by someone within the community. The same could be said of a pastor and a guest evangelist or speaker.

In some ways it is less threatening when given by an outsider. They are just visiting. The word may be true, but that outsider is not as personally involved in the past situation of the community, nor will he or she be present to see how the word is actually lived out in practical application. Somehow it is easier to accept a teaching from an outsider.

At the same time the outsider had better beware. If the teaching is too tough, they will say, how can he know what we need? After all, he isn't even one of us!

Why do we not accept the authority of those closer to us? Not only do they see us, we see them. Many times it is hard to accept the divine authority invested in someone who has grown up in ordinary life with us. We have seen them be just ordinary. How could they be so special now? Ironically, that which should comfort us in our local leaders, sometimes makes us quite uncomfortable.

Ultimately, we have to look not at the person with authority, but to ourselves. Many times we find any excuse possible to escape the authority of another. We are attracted to authority when it doesn't get too close. We are repelled from authority when it actually touches our own lives, especially when it asks us to change.

Today Jesus comes into our town. He comes as both a visitor and a local resident. In all cases he is asking us to change. He asks us to leave all and follow him. He asks us to give up sin. He asks us to become a disciple. How will we respond? Will we try to throw him out of town, or will we accept him? Will we be spellbound by his teaching, only to call out for crucifixion later, or will we become his disciple?   □

Forgiveness Breeds Repentance
Matthew 18:21-35 (3:Tuesday)

My heavenly Father will treat you in exactly the same way unless each of you forgives his brother from his heart. v. 35

What is the point of mercy? To bring people close to God so their life might prosper in the Lord. This is the good news, the gospel of Jesus Christ! When a person has been shown the truth and they repeatedly don't understand, sometimes the best thing to do is just drop it for a while. . . . Just wipe the slate clean and start over. Sometimes this is the best way to actually help them to accomplish the truth.

When a person is continually pressured, they can easily go from bad to worse. More guilt just breeds more failure, which breeds more guilt, and more failure and so on. It becomes a downward spiral of guilt and failure that leads to depression, despair, and death. The way to turn the spiral around and back up to God is through forgiveness. This relieves the pressure, gives the person some space, and allows them to try again. Many times they will now be able to succeed where they once were trapped in failure.

An even greater motivation for forgiveness is a brief look at ourselves. We must forgive as we have been forgiven, treat others the way we would like them to treat us, and to love our neighbor as ourself. Successful people would not be successful if they were held in too strict account for all their sins. God has been merciful. Even the greatest failure is not suffering the full consequence for sin. Even in failure we are given mercy. All of us have been treated mercifully by God who could easily exact justice for the sins of our soul. But he doesn't. He always gives us mercy. He always gives us another chance. Can we do otherwise?   □

Go the Extra Mile
Matthew 5:17-19 (3:Wednesday)

I have come, not to abolish them, but to fulfill them. v. 17

Today's Gospel reaffirms Jesus' support of the law of God. Many would depict Jesus as a radical revolutionary out to overthrow institutional religion and any objective concept of right or wrong concerning faith or morality. This simply doesn't jive with the words of Jesus himself. He never denied the law itself. He simply challenged the way the teachers of the law lived and taught it. It was only after the church spread to the Gentiles that the Jewish law was no longer mandatory for followers of Jesus.

It is important to remember that the heart of the law is mercy. The eye for the eye and the tooth for the tooth might seem harsh to us. When it was given, it was a way to moderate the vengeful pattern of Middle Eastern tribal life. Its intent was justice, but a justice moderated with mercy.

When Jesus teaches, he does not destroy the law. He surpasses it. He fulfills it by going beyond it. It is as if the "eye for the eye" of the law was God's way of keeping the door from slamming shut on humanity by moderating the prevailing violence of humankind. With Jesus the door is not simply propped open. It is swung totally open. The "eye for the eye" might well have propped open the door, but "turn the other cheek" swung the door open wide for good. The same could be said for all the teachings of Jesus in the Sermon on the Mount.

How well do we fulfill the minimal requirements of our law? The church too, must legislate on certain issues, but she always legislates to the lowest common denominator, to the least level of commitment. The same could be said of much of civil law. Do we simply fulfill the minimum, or do we fulfill it by far surpassing it? Today's Gospel teaches us to go beyond the more acceptable and go to the exceptional! Go the extra mile. Then you will fulfill not only the law, but the higher way of Jesus Christ himself.   □

Singleness of Heart
Luke 11:14-23 (3:Thursday)

Every kingdom divided against itself is laid waste. Any house torn by dissension falls. v. 17

Division is today's word of warning! St. Paul says, let there be no divisions among you. Jesus prays that we may be one so the world may believe. However, we are not united, so the world doesn't believe.

If the fifty million Catholic Christians in America were united, we could achieve a peaceful revolution in the United States at this crucial hour of world history. But we are not united. We openly disagree with church teachings on materialism and economics, the arms race, and the pro-life issues of abortion and artificial birth control. Consequently, there is no revolution.

Within our communities we must also be strongly united around a common vision and charism. Where there is not a strong and clear unity of ideals and purpose in a community, that community will fall.

On a more personal level, if there is not reconciliation after an offense between individual brothers and sisters, that community will fall apart. Jesus says that if you bring your gift to the altar and there remember that your brother or sister has something against you, go first to be reconciled before you offer your gift. Paul says not to let the sun go down on your wrath. Likewise, if your brother or sister has offended you in any way, or if you think you have offended them, you must go directly to them, not to someone else, to be reconciled.

Even more personally, we must check the unity of our heart. Is it divided? Jesus says blessed are the "pure" of heart. This word also means "clean" or "single." Our heart must be wholly undivided in its intention for God. If you want to check where your heart is, see where your mind goes when it wanders. Frequently, this will point out to you where your heart is still divided.

The word for purity is also used to describe winnowing the chaff from the wheat, or purifying metal by fire. These both purify. They are both active processes. Sometimes they can seem frightening and painful. Yet in the end, purity, cleanness, and sinlessness are the result.

Ultimately, it is Jesus who brings unity to division. It is Jesus who created the nations, who founded the churches, Jesus who raised up our communities, and Jesus who changes our heart. The more we center on Jesus and Jesus alone, the more united our whole life will become.

How divided are we today? Is our heart totally directed toward Jesus? Are our relationships reconciled in Jesus? Is our community and church vision centered in Jesus? If they are, we can revolutionize the whole world! □

Heart and Mind
Mark 12:28-34 (3:Friday)

"You shall love the Lord your God" . . . *"You shall love your neighbor as yourself." There is no other commandment greater than these.* vv. 30-31

What is love? Is it a feeling? Is it a decision? Or is it a decision of the heart and mind that includes and guides the feelings? I would conclude the latter.

Love is not just a feeling. If that were the case, you would love someone one day and hate them the next. Most married couples experience that a love based on emotional feelings alone is a love without foundation that leads to separation and divorce. Unfortunately, this is the kind of love embraced by most of modern society, as is evidenced by the staggering high statistics of divorce. Furthermore, this approach to love has filtered into the church as well, as is evidenced by the same statistics among those who call themselves Christian.

That doesn't mean that love is only a decision. A marital relationship that has no warmth or feeling is not really a marriage. It is only an arrangement. Granted, many such marriages have survived in the past. I once asked a respected married man of the Moslem faith if he loved his wife. He answered by asking what love had to do with marriage. His marriage had been arranged from his childhood by his parents. From all external perspectives this marriage had survived quite well. It was a decision and a decision alone. Feelings of love had nothing to do with it. But this is not ideal. It is not the highest definition of love.

I believe love is a decision that includes and guides the feelings. It can discern them and coincide with them. It can also stir them up and guide them when they are absent or negative.

Does our love for God and neighbor depend on the ebb

and flow of our feelings? Is our decision to love God and people relegated to a legalistic decision that never includes or affects our feelings? Do we know the proper way to discern and guide our feelings by our decision to love? The latter way is the most balanced and full. If you can learn how to love God and people in this way, you will fulfill the whole law and live an abundant and balanced life. Otherwise, you will find yourself unfulfilled by legalism or constantly torn up by emotionalism. □

Admit Your Sins
Luke 18:9-14 (3:Saturday)

O God, be merciful to me, a sinner. v. 13

The two men who went up to the temple to pray can teach us a lot about our approach to Christian living. One was a Pharisee. The other was a tax collector. The Pharisee did everything right from a theological perspective, but was not acceptable to God. The tax collector seemed to do everything wrong, but he went home justified before God.

The Pharisee was the member of an accepted renewal group within the Jewish faith. They believed all the right things, even by later Christian standards. They believed in the eternal life of the human spirit, as opposed to the belief of the Sadducees who didn't believe in everlasting life. They believed in a justification by faith where God looked to the intentions of the heart, rather than the mere fulfillment of external ritual of the law, though they were strict about external fulfillment.

They even believed all the right things about the Messiah. They knew where and when he would be born. They knew he would teach as no man had taught before. They knew he would be rejected by the religious leaders of his day. They knew he would die by Roman crucifixion. They knew he would rise on the third day and give his Spirit to all nations, not just the Jewish people. They knew all this "correct" doctrine, yet still missed Jesus.

Today's Pharisee does everything right. He boldly approaches God's throne of grace. He gives God all the thanks, praise, and glory for any of his accomplishments. He thanks God that he is not like the tax collector, yet he does not go home justified.

The tax collector was seen as the lowest of the low by the orthodox Jew. The tax collector was usually a Jew who had betrayed his own people by working for the Roman occupation. Furthermore, he grew rich by cheating his own people, and was famous for immoral living among prostitutes and whores. Yet, the tax collector went home from the temple justified. Why? He made no pretense of holiness. He simply confessed his sin and honestly begged God's forgiveness. The Pharisee made an art of hiding behind his theology.

What about us? Do we have the honesty of the tax collector in confessing our own sins? Or have we developed our theology into an artful illusion about our own sin? Be honest before God. Admit your sins and your success. Don't hide behind either. Then you will be justified by God. □

Signs and Wonders
John 4:43-54 (4:Monday)

Unless you people see signs and wonders, you do not believe. v. 48

Why does God give us signs and wonders? The first reason is answered in today's Gospel. Unless we see signs and wonders, we will not believe. The second reason has to do with the nature of God himself. God usually chooses to work within the laws of the universe he created, but he doesn't have to. God is infinite and beyond any created limitation. The extraordinary, the miraculous, is simply a part of God's being.

Today's Gospel definitely gives us a negative connotation to the words of Jesus Christ in regard to seeking signs and wonders. Yes, God might work through them to initially establish faith and periodically structure it, but he doesn't want us to stay overly dependent on them.

What are the things that will last when all the charismatic signs and wonders pass away? St. Paul tells us in his great discourse on charismatic gifts that faith, hope, and love will last forever, and "the greatest of these is love" (1 Cor 13:13).

Faith is not a feeling. It is a decision. Faith is believing beyond seeing. We walk by faith and not by sight. Jesus only had as much faith as he possessed in the Garden of Gethsemani. He did not feel like being faithful. He didn't want to die, but he did anyway. Because of this obedient faith, God raised him up on the third day.

Likewise, we only have as much hope as we have in the most hopeless moment. It may seem hopeless, but by faith we know that it is not. Faith gives us hope. Yet without hope, we will soon lose our faith.

Furthermore, we only have as much love as we possess for our greatest enemy. Jesus says love your enemy and pray for your persecutor. It is easy to love those who love us, or at least do not actively abuse us. But it is difficult to love your persecutor and your active enemy.

Do we really love? Do we really hope? Do we really have faith? If not, do not give up! We can still change. We can still grow. In the end it is these virtues that really evangelize the world. The world has seen signs and wonders, but it doesn't change. The world can still see more virtue from us. We can still change more. Then maybe the world will believe! ☐

Healing Hullabaloo
John 5:1-3, 5-16 (4:Tuesday)

"Do you want to be healed?"... "It is the Sabbath and you are not allowed to carry that mat around." The man who had been restored to health had no idea who it was [who cured him]. vv. 6, 10, 13

There are three major points that strike me today: Do we really want to be healed? Do we overly structure healing? Do we want to be noticed by healing others?

Jesus asks the sick man today, "Do you want to be healed?" The same could be asked of us. Sometimes sickness gets us things: attention, time off, needed rest. I would even go so far as to say that God sometimes uses sickness to force us into some of these things. Ideally, though, we should be finding them in better ways. Sometimes we are just being self-indulgent in our somatic or psychosomatic tendencies toward sickness.

Jesus will not usually heal us unless we really want to be healed. We must believe that what we ask for in prayer will happen, with no inner doubts, or it will not. If we don't really want to be healed in the first place, we will be filled with inner doubts, and we will not be healed.

Do we overly structure religion so that it excludes healing? The Sabbath laws quoted by the Jews in today's Gospel were not God's, they were man's. They were of human origin. Oh yes, the Old Testament law concerning work on the Sabbath had inspired their law, but now they were impeding the greater divine law by their human precepts.

Sometimes we do the same. The sacrament of the anointing of the sick was given by God, but sometimes we limit God to the sacrament he gave and thus discount healings through other non-sacramental means. Yes, there should be discretion and discernment. The integrity of the sacraments should be retained, but to limit God to the law he gave is to attempt to control and monopolize God. This is the worst arrogance.

Lastly, who gets the honor for healing? Jesus doesn't seek glory for this healing. The sick man didn't even know who healed him. How different are the "faith healers" of today! They are always center stage with the cameras rolling. Jesus slips through the crowd without even being recognized. Do we seek recognition in our ministry? If so, then it is not really Christian.

To conclude, we ask the same three questions: Do we really want healing? Do we limit God's healing by human laws? Do we really give God glory for healing? How we answer these questions may give us insight about the effectiveness or ineffectiveness of the healing ministry in our community, church, or ministry team. □

Learn from Examples
John 5:17-30 (4:Wednesday)

The Son cannot do anything by himself—he can do only what he sees the Father doing. v. 19

Jesus didn't do anything in his life or ministry that he did not learn from the Father: He did absolutely nothing "on his own." Because of that, he becomes a pattern and example for others. What about our life today? Do we still want to do things on our own? Anything not intentionally patterned on Christ cannot really be called "Christian."

How did Jesus learn the ways of the Father? The first way is through personal example. Jesus pre-existed with the

Father from eternity. He had a lot of time to learn! Second, while he sojourned on earth, he prayed. He did not pray selfishly. It was not "his time." It was God's time! There he put aside his own will and conformed to the will of the Father. So Jesus learned the ways of the Father through example and through prayer.

How do we learn the ways of Jesus? In much the same way. First, we learn from the Spirit who is stirred up in prayer. The true Spirit can only teach what he has first learned from the Son. This is not "my time." It is God's! It involves the sacrifice of the schoolroom. In prayer we learn how to become more like Jesus.

Second, we learn through life in the church. Jesus chose the apostles, who in turn made provisions for the leaders who would follow them in the early church. Jesus said to the apostles that those who accepted them, accepted him; and those who rejected them, rejected Christ. Because of this, those like St. Ignatius of Antioch could also say that those who rejected the bishop rejected Christ. A succession of teaching authority and example was passed on from Christ to the whole church. It still ripples out from Christ to us today in the church.

There is another succession we can learn from. It is the succession of the saints. If we want to find out how to live the radical gospel of Jesus today, we can learn much from the rich tradition of saints who have done the same for the last two thousand years: St. Francis and Clare, St. John of the Cross and Theresa of Avila, St. Benedict and Scholastica, St. Antony of the Desert and Macrina, just to name a few. If we hear them, we hear Christ. If we reject them, we reject Christ. For those interested in the more radical way of gospel living, the saints show us much concerning the way of Christ.

What about the Gospels themselves? They were given through the church to point the way to Christ. They became the most basic rule of life for the saints. If we want to find out how Jesus lived, read the Gospels. Then don't excuse yourself.

What about us today? How does our life compare to the above examples? If you are not a saint, you can be! If you are not like Christ, you can be! Anything that is not like Christ and his saints must be rejected. Otherwise we risk rejecting Christ! □

Mine Our Gold
John 5:31-47 (4:Thursday)

If you believed Moses you would then believe me, ... But if you do not believe what he wrote, how can you believe what I say? vv. 46-47

Today we deal with simple belief in the bare words and gospel of Jesus Christ. For many this is not enough. It must be "dressed up" with the newest spiritual teaching or religious trip.

This is relevant to the recent incorporation of Eastern religion into Christianity. Recently, the church has spoken an official warning against an excessive incorporation of Eastern non-Christian practices into the monastic and contemplative centers of the church in particular. What should our approach be?

First, it should be understood that certain truths that come from non-Christian origins can be "baptized," or purged of that which is incompatible with Jesus, and used in the Christian life. No doubt, there are certain human and divine realities that non-Christian religions share with Christians. In Eastern meditation, for instance, there are at least certain psychological realities Christian meditation shares in common. Likewise, some of their experiences in these areas might actually be more developed than ours. This is not because we do not possess the fullness already in Christ. It is because we have not used what we already possess.

What about the pastoral level? Things might seem acceptable, but pastorally, many are still dangerous. The emphasis on Eastern meditation and psychological self-awareness has often not made people more like Christ. It has just made them selfish. Oh yes, they meditate and pray, but they do not really worship Jesus. They may even paint his name over everything they do. But essentially nothing has changed. It is still centered on self.

Jesus' words stand in stark contrast to the typical experience of incorporating Eastern mysticism into Christianity. Jesus says you find yourself by losing yourself. He says you find wealth in poverty. Life in death. St. Francis' or Mother Teresa's washing of a leper's sores is more "prayerful" than hours of "centering" in the self. This is a major difference between the stark words of Christ and the various Eastern trips in which we try to dress them up. The stark words of Jesus are far more fulfilling.

Of course, we must avoid the overly wary "watch out" mentality. Some Christians have even gone so far as to counsel against classical Christian meditation and contemplation in their paranoias about Eastern religions and New Age. We need response. Not reaction. If we respond from the wealth of our own Christian tradition, we will have more than enough mysticism to go around. The Christian traditions of meditation and contemplation are just as rich, if not more so, than that found in any other religion. The saints show us the way. Why look around the world when there is already a gold mine in your own back yard?   □

A Costly Statement
John 7:1-2, 10, 25-30 (4:Friday)

So you know me, and you know my origins? v. 28

There is an apparent and a hidden reality going on in the Gospel today: "Come to Jerusalem. Show yourself. Nobody is trying to kill you." That is the apparent. The hidden reality is just the opposite. Jesus sees it clearly while nobody else does. Ironically, they accuse Jesus of being hidden, while in truth, it is they who are still hiding.

Jesus comes from his Father in heaven. He claims that most of his religious listeners are actually born of the father of lies, the devil. Both claim to be of God. One is obviously wrong. Jesus goes on to say that those born of the devil actually cannot hear him. Only those born of God are even capable of hearing his voice. To those not born of God, his voice and his words are silent within their hearts. They simply cannot relate.

Jesus is aware of this hidden reality. The others are not. For them they simply judge by apparent reality. From this perspective things can seem fine when, in fact, they are not. All that is required is conformity. Had Jesus just played along, obeyed the externals of the law, and spoken in a little less inflammatory manner, he would have been fine.

But Jesus went too far. He was interested in spiritual unity, not just religious conformity. He spoke to the internal as well as to the external. He knew those who were of a different spirit and was not afraid to say so. He knew and obeyed the spirit of the law even when it meant amending the miniscule details of the human interpretation of the law by religious commentators and lawmakers. This put him at odds with many of the religious people of the day, even those who had gained a place of authority.

What about us? Do we judge by the externals or the internals? Are we interested in unity, or just conformity? Are we willing to speak out against a bad spirit in our midst, or do we simply keep quiet to keep the peace when all the rules are at least being minimally obeyed? You might get by with the minimum and even gain a place of authority in this world, but it may cost you your soul. It was not the way of Jesus Christ. He spoke out for the higher call. It cost him his life. Are you willing to do the same?   □

God Speaks to the Soul
John 7:40-50 (4:Saturday)

No man ever spoke like that before. v. 46

No man has ever spoken the way Jesus spoke. Oh yes, there had been teachers. Oh yes, there had been prophets. Oh yes, there had been holy men before. But no one before or since has spoken like Jesus.

Jesus' words got down into the soul. They went beyond the mind and got right to the heart. They didn't deny the mind. They simply surpassed it. They came forth from the soul of God and went to the soul of all humankind. They would not be limited to a mere understanding of the mind. They required a response from the whole human soul.

As such, Jesus' words surpassed the greatest intellectuals, yet were understandable by the littlest of children. So it has always been. The few and simple written words of Jesus have challenged theologians, philosophers, lawyers, psychologists, doctors, and scientists to fill the libraries of the world with commentaries on his words. Yet none of them has ever grasped his words as completely as the heart of a child. So it should be. Jesus should satisfy and surpass the intellectual longings of the whole human race, yet without ever surpassing the simplicity of a child.

The Middle Easterner sees words as the extension of the soul. They are not just intellectual tools. They are an expression of the whole human soul. Thus, when Jesus is seen as the Word of God incarnate, he is the incarnation of God's soul. Such a Word can only be grasped by the human soul which itself reflects the image of God. If you try to hold it in the mind, it will elude you. God's soul must be grasped in the human soul. Otherwise, the real meaning of God's Word is lost.

Today's Gospel shows theologians who are incapable of understanding Jesus because they have become trapped into trying to understand God in the mind alone. Those who understand Jesus are the simple and the uneducated. They are less conditioned by human theology. They understand God because for them it is not a science of study . . . an "ology." It is life.

There is also Nicodemus . . . , the theologian, the Pharisee, the member of the Sanhedrin. Somehow Nicodemus' heart is still alive. His theology has awakened his heart. He is still open to Jesus. He is not far from the kingdom of God.

Are we like the typical philosopher, or are we like the blessed Nicodemus? Are we like the scientists or like the simple? Jesus comes to fulfill the longings of the mind and far surpasses this limited human capacity to reach the heart. It is on them that the New Covenant is most fully written. □

A Second Chance
John 8:1-11 (5:Monday)

Let the man among you who has no sin be the first to cast a stone at her. v. 7

Today's Gospel teaches us justice and mercy. It also shows us the way to the higher justice of mercy.

In today's story a woman is caught in the act of adultery. She is not being falsely charged. She is guilty. She has actually been caught in the act, probably by her own husband.

The Old Testament law is very clear about this. She must be stoned to death. She must die. Of course, it can be argued that the point of the law was to moderate the unjust vengeance of the ancient era, where entire tribes war with one another over such incidents. Likewise, it could be argued that under Roman occupation the Jews could not carry out capital punishment. That was reserved for the authority of Roman justice alone. But these are peripheral arguments. Both Jesus and his opponents knew the issue; Would Jesus agree with the clear teaching of the Old Testament law?

Jesus does not disagree with the law. He questions those who execute it. He doesn't question the concept of justice. He heightens our sensitivity to justice. In the long run this brings mercy.

The essence of Jesus' response is this: "Let you without sin cast the first stone." Who is without sin? Jesus had taught that anyone who even looks lustfully at another person is already guilty of adultery. Who has not committed such a sin? Who has not gone on and actually committed at least some greater sin in the flesh? Yet God has forgiven us our sin. Some of these sins are never publicly exposed. They are known only to us and God. Who then can condemn another according to justice? Jesus says to treat others the way you would have them treat you. Jesus and Paul say to forgive others the way God has forgiven you. This is the point of today's story.

This does not mean we are to whitewash sin. Jesus does not condemn the woman caught in adultery. He does warn her: "Go your way and sin no more." Forgiveness is not an excuse to sin. It is a second chance from God.

In the end the choice is yours. God gives you the power to overcome sin. He gives forgiveness. He gives the truth to guide you. He gives the Spirit to empower you. If you want you can overcome sin. That is the end result of forgiveness. □

Silence and Spoken Words
John 8:21-30 (5:Tuesday)

I could say much to you in condemnation, but no, I only tell the world what I have heard from him, the truthful One who sent me. v. 26

When should we speak, and when should we be silent? When have we spoken too much or not enough? How do we learn the difference? Today's Gospel answers these questions for us.

Jesus said that there was much he could speak to the world about condemnation, but he doesn't speak these words. He says that he only speaks the words he hears from his Father in heaven. He doesn't speak everything he knows.

Jesus also says that there is much more that he could say, but we would not be able to bear it now. What he would say would be true. It would have much to do with great spiritual mysteries. He knows that we could not be able to bear the full revelation of these truths, so he is silent. He knows his listeners. He is able to gauge how much to speak by knowing his audience.

The Scriptures are filled with admonitions concerning the pursuit of wisdom. But for all my searching for what constitutes that wisdom, I have found one essential thing: knowing when to speak and when to be silent. Beyond the beginning step of the fear of the Lord, this is the most concrete thing I can find. Knowing this is the mark of true wisdom.

Out of all the Scriptures, I have narrowed it down to this: Always be willing to be silent, then you can safely speak. Never use silence as an escape from the responsibility of speaking the truth. The balance of these two statements keeps me pretty much on track. Of course, in our sinful humanity, we will never get it as perfect as Jesus, and we may not always know what to speak when we must. This is part of the tension of simply being human.

How do we learn the truth we must sometimes speak? Through Scripture. Through the teaching of the church. Neither of these ways will do any good if we do not seek the enlightenment of the Holy Spirit who leads us into all truth. How do we seek the Spirit? Through taking definite times of long and intense prayer.

Today learn two lessons: the lessons of silence and solitude. If you take time for silence, you will learn what to speak. If you take time for solitude, you will learn when and where to speak it. □

What Is Truth?
John 8:31-42 (5:Wednesday)

You will know the truth, and the truth will set you free. v. 32

Jesus says that you will know the truth and the truth will set you free. Pilate later asks him, "What is the truth?" In a different place Jesus says that he himself is "the way, the truth, and the life" (Jn 8:32; 18:38).

We too are sometimes confused about the truth. Like Pilate, we come from a world of many opinions. Like Pilate, we come face to face with Jesus. We too have to make a decision about the truth of Jesus Christ.

It seems to me that there are two major errors in Christendom in approaching the truth. There is also a third way that is correct.

The first error is an undue liberalism that makes God in an image of a human being . . . including sin. How do we find the truth of God? Simply take a vote, and the majority wins! Right? Wrong! If we had done this in various points of Christendom history, the church would not hold to some basic and essential points of faith and morality we now take almost for granted. The church is not a pure democracy. It is a theocracy.

The second error is the undue fundamentalism that wants a black and white answer to everything. It is found either in the Scripture or the magisterium all the time. This approach to faith and morality takes all the subtle tones and shades from the face of Christ. Instead of his face looking alive through a combination of black, white, and subtle shades and colors, it is reduced to a cartoon.

The third way understands the difference between the written law and the Word incarnate. In the Old Testament God sent us a letter. In the New Testament God paid us a personal visit in Jesus. Jesus came in human flesh and gathered human disciples. He personally chose apostles as leaders and breathed the Spirit on them for their ministry. Then he poured the Spirit on all believers at Pentecost after his death, resurrection, and ascension. These apostles raised up churches as they spread the good news everywhere. It was out of this living experience of the incarnate Word that the New Testament was written and compiled. If we want to understand this truth, we cannot separate the Scriptures from the church. The authority of Scripture builds on the authority of the church.

How does this affect you and me? If you want to know the

truth of Christ, consult the New Testament, the magisterium of the church, *and* consult the lives of the saints! If you want to find out how to follow Jesus radically today, consult those who have done so before. Consult the saints! If you have a question about matters such as doctrine or sacraments, consult the saints. You will hear a chorus of orthodoxy in reply. If you want to know about chastity, or obedience, or poverty, consult the saints. You will hear a unanimous response like a chorus of the angels of God. Once you hear this response, be humble enough to change. Bend your will and your opinions to a truth that is living and clear. It is the truth of Jesus Christ. It is a truth that will set you free.   □

Are We Ready?
John 8:51-59 (5:Thursday)

I solemnly declare it: before Abraham came to be, I AM. **v. 58**

This morning the tension mounts and breaks in the great Johannine drama between Jesus and his religious inter-rogators. Both claim to be from God. Both claim the other is of the devil. Jesus says that they are of their father, the devil. They say Jesus is demon possessed. Finally, Jesus breaks the tension by "upping the odds" to an unthinkable height: He actually calls himself God, the great I AM. At this, the Jews take up stones and actually try to kill Jesus. The tension breaks. All comes clear. Yes, they are trying to kill Jesus. Yes, Jesus claims not just to be *of* God, but to be God himself.

Why is it so unthinkable to call yourself I AM? When God first revealed himself to Moses, he called himself "I AM that I AM." God meant that he is underived existence. He is wholly other. He is transcendent, beyond concepts of space and time or any of the characters of creation at all.

For God to be I AM means that he is beyond the concepts of the past or the future. God simply is. He exists in the past, the present, and the future all at once. Time and space are part of creation. God is not bound to them unless he chooses to be.

For Jesus to be I AM is considered blasphemy by the orthodox Jews. How could he, a human being, be beyond these concepts and confines of creation? It was ludicrous! He had to be either insane, demon possessed, or both. On the other hand, perhaps what he said was true. What Jesus is claiming is to be the incarnate I AM. Yes, he is temporarily bound by time and space by his own choice, but the essence of his being is still united with his Father through the Spirit.

What about us? We too are now seated with Christ at the right hand of the Father through the Spirit. There is part of us already existing in eternity. Our spirit knows this in the Spirit of God, while our soul and body continue in pilgrimage in created space and time.

Are we really aware of eternity? Do we walk on earth in a way that is affected by these mysteries of eternity? We should. Better yet, we can. If we keep our eyes on the eternal, we will become more effective in the here and now. If we are ready to live in the present moment, we will be really ready for eternity. Like Jesus, we are to dwell in and with the I AM. Like Jesus, we must still walk the face of this earth. This leads us to Calvary. This leads us to the empty tomb. Eventually, this leads us to ascend from our own Mount of Olives to heaven. Are we really ready? □

We Reflect God
John 10:31-42 (5:Friday)

"You who are only a man are making yourself God." Jesus answered: "Is it not written in your law, 'I have said, you are gods'?" vv. 33-34

Jesus has finally done it! He has clearly proclaimed himself as God. He says it clearly. It is understood by his listeners clearly. Their response is again clear. They try to kill him.

Yesterday we spoke of Jesus as the incarnate I AM. We also recognized that in Christ we share in this aspect of the eternal and the divine.

Today Jesus speaks very clearly about the divine mystery at work in human beings. Today he quotes the Old Testament Scripture that says, "You are gods." We are different than the rest of creation. Creation may bear God's traces, but the human being reflects God's image. Both in creation and redemption the divine is at work in the human in a most special way.

How do we respond to this divine gift? Are we really aware of the divine realities at work within our own human soul?

It should evoke a real reverence in our soul for human life. Yes, we are to reverence all life, for it bears the traces of the living God. But this mystery calls us to an extraordinary reverence for human life in particular. In reverencing the human, we reverence the divine. In reverencing people, we reverence God.

Before we get all excited about the "glories" of this revelation, we had better look closer at today's Gospel and the Lenten season in which it is read. Jesus' revelation of his divinity does not bring him glory. It brings him humiliation and painful death. This approach to divinity is not some kind of New Age attempt for self-glorification. It brings us face-to-face with the mundane, hum-drum, and even extraordinary sorrowful and painful realities of human existence. If we cannot face these human realities and reverence them as divine gifts, then we are not really entering into the divine.

Today we are called to two aspects of growth and reverence in the divine life in Christ. One: We are called to grow in the glorious mysteries of the eternal at work in our own soul. Two: We are called to fully enter into the mundane realities of human existence in limited space and time.

God wants to expand our limited vision to the extreme left and right. He wants to remove our blinders of mediocrity. Some of us are called to see more glory than ever before. Some are called to enter more fully into human sorrow. Some are called to see both at once in a mystical flash of intuition. All of us are called to stretch and grow. We do this by cooperating with God's grace rather than resisting it, no matter which area of growth we are in right now.

Are you ready to grow? Are you ready to share in the divine life? Are you ready to follow the way of Jesus Christ? Are you ready to reverence?   □

Who's in Control?
John 11:45-57 (5:Saturday)

Can you not see that it is better for you to have one man die than to have the whole nation destroyed? v. 50

How well do we cooperate with the sovereign action of God? How well do we see the action of God through both the good and the evil of the world? Do we really believe that God is in control? These are the questions raised by today's Gospel.

In today's Gospel Caiaphas thinks he is defeating Jesus. Actually, he is helping fulfill the plans of Jesus. Ironically, he also thinks he is doing God's will by opposing this "heretic." Really he is only cooperating with God's sovereign will by playing out the role of God's enemy so that God can eventually show himself victorious.

Furthermore, he is actually prophesying a truth of God's redemption of Israel while not really understanding what he was saying. This is part of the mystery of good, evil, and the sovereignty of God.

I believe this mystery is best explained by the language of God's perfect will and God's permission. God's perfect will is always to the highest good. Some speak further of God's imperfect will that allows a good that is not the highest good. This is a matter of good and better. Then there is the matter of good and evil. There is the matter of God actually permitting temporary evil so that a higher and more long lasting good can be accomplished. This means that God is in control even of the evil that is trying to oppose him. He never wills evil, but he does allow it. Furthermore, he uses evil to defeat itself and accomplish good. This is good news! God is in control!

What about us? Are we really able to remain faithful and hopeful even in the midst of terrible evil? If we believe that God is working out sovereign will even in the midst of evil, we will remain faithful and hopeful. If we do not really believe this, then we could easily lose hope and faith. Do we really believe this mystery? Jesus did! That is why he was able to face even death on a cross. He believed there would be a resurrection. □

Costly Worship
John 12:1-11 (Holy Week:Monday)

Mary brought a pound of costly perfume . . . with which she anointed Jesus' feet. Then she dried them with her hair. v. 3

There are two main points today. How do we prepare the house of God externally? How do we prepare the house of our soul?

Today's Western churches have largely become monuments to a utilitarian Christianity. We spend millions on sound and lights, but our churches are devoid of sign and symbol. Liturgy is almost nonexistent. We have reduced worship of Jesus to a rock concert or a popular stage show. Granted, we must use the things of a culture to reach a culture. However, now it seems that Christianity is more affected by Western culture, than Christianity is actually affecting the West. This is symbolized in the actual buildings in which we worship.

Jesus was from the Middle East. He was a Jew. The worship of the Middle East was rich with sign and symbol. It was highly liturgical. This was because they believed that God worked in and through creation in a way greater than the experience of only one person. Their sign and symbol was both simple and rich, personal and corporate.

Jesus never once spoke out against this kind of worship. He only spoke against its abuse. He gives us every indication that he participated in all the liturgical worship of the Jews. Jesus simply spoke against that which was entered into vainly, without the understanding of the heart. The early church followed Jesus' example by developing its own liturgy and celebration of sacraments. The worship of the first disciples was far more liturgical and sacramental than the utilitarian approach to worship and spirituality so common in our modern Western churches. Those who oppose the use of rich sign and symbol in worship are more akin to Judas than to Jesus, according to the words of today's Gospel.

Yet it is much more than just a lesson about liturgy and sacraments. There is a lesson about the heart. We must bring Jesus not only the costly perfumes of common worship through liturgy and sacrament. We must bring him the costly perfumes of the soul. We must bring him that part of our life we value even beyond cost. It might be very private and personal. Nobody might know of it but you and God, but that is the perfume you must anoint Jesus' feet with today.

Furthermore, Mary wiped the feet of Jesus with her hair. She did not use a towel. She used her hair. Hair is again very personal. It is part of our "look," our self-image. Mary sacrificed her hair in worship of Jesus. She sacrificed her self-image, her beauty. It was deeply personal. Can we do the same?

Do our churches look more like civic auditoriums than like houses of worship? Do we really believe that God works through creation in a way that is holy? More importantly, are we willing to spend the most costly area of our soul in order to worship Jesus? Do we wipe his feet with a towel, or are we willing to use our hair?   □

The Deep Despair of Judas
John 13:21-33, 36-38 (Holy Week:Tuesday)

I tell you solemnly, one of you will betray me. v. 21

The Gospel asks us to consider two people today. They are Judas and Simon Peter. Both deny the Lord. Both respond to that denial differently. Only one is saved.

Judas Iscariot is commonly known as Jesus' betrayer. He is seen as demon-possessed and devious, the incarnation of evil. While it is true that the Gospel today says that the devil actually entered into Judas, this did not happen until the very end. Up until now Judas has been trying to follow Jesus like the rest. Even at the Last Supper he is not actually aware that he is betraying Christ. He asks, "You don't mean me?"

with all the rest when Jesus says one will betray him.

Simon Peter's denial was actually more obvious. He flatly denies having ever known Jesus at all! What is this if not a betrayal of loyalty? What makes it worse is that Peter is one of the three who made up the closest to Jesus among the twelve. Furthermore, he was given a special and unique place of leadership among the twelve by Christ himself. Later on this would have vast ramifications in the leadership of the whole church throughout the ages. However, today this makes Peter all the more responsible and all the more guilty. I wonder, sin for sin, whose was actually worse, Peter's or Judas'?

It is not the extent of the sin that decides their eventual salvation. It is their response to sin. Judas is sorry for his betrayal, but he does not repent. He ends in despair and suicide, hanging himself from a tree. Peter is also sorry, but Peter repents. He turns back to Jesus. Because of this Peter goes on as the chief apostle in the early church. Judas is remembered only for his sin.

What about us? We too will betray Christ at times. We too will eventually deny him. That is not the question. The question is how we will respond to our own sin. Will we despair or will we repent? Sorrow is not enough. Change is required. If we repent of sin, we will be saved. If we only feel sorry and stay in despair, we will be lost. The message of Jesus' gospel remains ever the same: Repent and believe the good news! □

Judas, "Leadership Material"
Matthew 26:14-25 (Holy Week:Wednesday)

The man who has dipped his hand into the dish with me is the one who will hand me over. v. 23

Yesterday we considered Judas and Peter. Today we do the same. Yesterday we considered their response to their denial of Christ. Today we must look from another perspective. We must look from the perspective of their closeness to Jesus.

Some of the symbolic customs of the Passover meal were signs of closeness and intimacy. That is what we look for today. One of these would include the washing of the guests' hands or feet. Jesus offers this to all and goes beyond the usually accepted hand-washing and washes all their feet. In this he calls them all friends and calls himself the servant of all.

There is also a significance in Jesus' sop with Judas. To sop meat or bread and hand it to a guest was a symbol of special closeness and honor for the guest. John's Gospel portrays Jesus' sop with Judas as one of this kind. This meant Jesus was actually giving special honor and friendship to his betrayer, Judas. It was a common symbol and understood by all.

Some have also commented on the seating arrangement. Some believe Judas had actually been seated in the guest place of honor next to Jesus. This made their sopping from the same dish possible as depicted by Matthew's and Mark's Gospels. Some say Peter had perhaps sulked a bit and in sarcastic symbolism taken the lowest place directly across the room from Jesus. This would actually enable Jesus to speak most clearly to Peter about his denials. He was directly across from Jesus.

All of this brings out the closeness of Judas to Jesus. He was not a distant disciple. He was very close to the person and mission of Jesus. He was considered trustworthy enough to take care of the common purse. Perhaps he was even considered "leadership material" from a certain perspective. He was, after all, an apostle. He was one of the twelve.

How do we handle our intimacy with Jesus? Yesterday we discussed our denials of Christ. Today we discuss our closeness to Christ. Both are a part of the Christian experience. So the question is not will you be close to him, or will you deny him. The question is how you handle yourself in both situations. Furthermore, we must ask how we handle ourselves as Christian leaders or administrators. All of us are called to lead at something sooner or later. Here again we can look to either Peter, the rock, or Judas Iscariot. The choice remains before us all. Will we be Peter or will we be Judas? ☐

The New Passover
John 13:1-15 (Holy Week:Holy Thursday)

Jesus—rose from the meal and took off his cloak. vv. 3-4

The Lord's Supper, the Eucharist, is the celebration of the new Passover. It remembers the new and final sacrifice of the Paschal Lamb, Jesus the Lord. Jesus did not invent the Lord's Supper. He built the new on the foundation of the old. He instituted the Lord's Supper in the midst of the traditional Passover meal of the Jews.

The Passover meal involved four cups of wine and three matzos, or unleavened bread, plus the paschal lamb, *haroses* or bitter herbs, green herbs dipped in salt water, and *moror*, or a paste of fruit and bitter seasoning. These all had special significance for the Jews, based on the Exodus from the slavery of Egypt to freedom.

The first cup was used in the *Kiddish,* or opening blessing. Jesus said that after it he would not drink of the fruit of the vine again until he drank it with them in the kingdom. This was not the same cup used as the cup of his blood. The *Kiddish* also involved the eating of green herbs dipped in salt water to remind the Jewish people of their sorrow in Egypt.

Next came the *Hagadah,* or story of their deliverence, in the reading of Exodus 12, the questions by the youngest, and the explanation given by the elder about the Exodus. The meaning of the various foods set before them were explained. Wine was a symbol of God's providential care from the earth; unleavened bread, a symbol of bread baked in the haste of departure; bitter herbs, the symbol of the bitterness of slavery; *moror,* the symbol of the bricks and mortar the Jews made under harsh slavery. Most importantly, the paschal lamb was a symbol of the lamb eaten in sacrifice and the blood put on doorposts of their houses so the angel of death would "pass over" their houses as God showed his ninth plague to Pharaoh. Jesus kept all this unchanged.

After that came the singing of the psalms, or songs of thanksgiving for deliverance. The meal was then solemnly blessed. At this point, a second cup of wine was drunk and a matzo broken and eaten along with the above mentioned dishes, save the lamb. This was still not the Lord's Supper, the Eucharist.

After the solemn blessing the paschal meal was consumed. This was a normal meal eaten in celebration and memorial of the freedom of the Jews from Egypt.

Next, after the supper, came a third cup of wine and a second matzo. This was where Jesus instituted the Lord's Supper. Here, after fulfilling the essence of the Passover meal in obedience to Old Testament Scripture, Jesus used the remainder of the service to symbolize something new . . . the sacrifice of himself as the eternal Paschal Lamb to bring all people from slavery to sin into spiritual freedom; he gave his own body and blood in death to bring life to all. This was the Christian Eucharist.

At the very end came the fourth cup of blessing. This is the cup of Melchizedek, an eternal priest who, according to legend in Scripture, had no earthly origins or parents.

We can see three distinct symbols: our link with the Jewish people from whom Jesus came forth; our link with the Catholic church which spread out beyond the limits of one race to all nations through a "common union" called Communion, or Eucharist; our link with each other in Christ in communities raised up by the wind of the Spirit. Tonight we thank God for all three realities.   □

A Great Love
John 18:1; 19:42 (Holy Week:Good Friday)

Jesus went out with his disciples across the Kidron Valley. v. 1

The journey from the Upper Room to Calvary is long. The long liturgical readings of the Passion are meant to give us a taste of that journey.

The journey begins at Gethsemani, a garden east of the city across the Kidron Valley. Here Jesus goes with his eleven remaining apostles to spend the night. He asks Peter, James, and John to stay awake and pray with him for one hour. In light of the long paschal supper with its four cups of strong wine and many courses of food, they find this nearly impossible and fall asleep. Jesus prays alone. He goes through such mental and emotional anguish that he sweats drops of blood, a condition that betrays almost complete emotional breakdown and leaves the nerves of the skin hypersensitive to touch of any kind. Jesus prays for the Father to let this cup pass, but ends by saying, "Thy will be done." He is then betrayed and arrested.

Jesus is taken across the Kidron Valley to Caiaphas the high priest on the far side of the city. There is a night session of the Sanhedrin. After the mock trial, a trial for which he is emotionally too drained to properly face, he is imprisoned in a hole that can only be entered by lowering the criminal down by rope. This is where the exhausted Jesus spent the few remaining hours before daybreak.

In the morning, Jesus is sent on foot to the other far side of the city to the Antonio Fortress where Pilate and the Roman garrison resided. In an attempt to escape the embarrassing predicament between Jesus' obvious innocence and the hatred of the Jews, Pilate sends Jesus to Herod. So again Jesus is marched to another far side of the city.

Herod's soldiers beat Jesus and Herod toys with Jesus. After Herod can find no guilt in Jesus, he sends him back to Pilate . . . another walk in exhaustion and pain across the city.

Now the abuse begins in earnest. First, Jesus is whipped just short of death by the Romans. His backside is left a shredded, bloody mess. After the whipping, the soldiers dressed the accused in a king's robe, crowned him with thorns, and mocked him.

The convict was then stripped of the cloak that, no doubt, stuck to his skin in dried blood and made to carry a cross beam of about one hundred pounds a few thousand feet to a place on a hill outside the city where criminals were crucified, named Golgotha, or the place of the skull. Jesus was no doubt walking in a state of shock. Tradition has it that he fell three times. Scripture mentions once. It could easily have been more.

On Calvary, according to normal Roman custom, Jesus was now thrown on his shredded back, nailed to the crossbeam through his wrists, and hoisted onto the stationary upright beam. His feet were then nailed to a foot rest. This caused extreme pain. The nails in his wrists went through the central nerves of each arm, sending hot, shooting pain down both arms and causing repeated muscle cramps and uncontrollable contractions throughout his chest, back, and arms. He beat himself up against the cross with his shredded back in uncontrollable spasms and muscle contractions. Furthermore, he began to suffocate, for due to his posture and the cramps, he could breathe in but not out. Only by putting weight on his nailed feet could he raise himself enough to either breathe or speak. His last words were of great effort through great pain. Eventually this posture causes a chain reaction of suffocation and heart attack. Most scholars believe that Jesus' heart burst before

nis would have been one last intense and
e he died.

erienced all the darkness and pain of all
emotional and spiritual level in one day. He
and bore our sorrows.

ugh it all out of love. Had you or I been the
only living soul to believe, he would still have done it all.
How can we now not respond to his love?   □

Christ Is Risen!
Day: John 20:1-9 or Matthew 28:1-10
Evening: Luke 29:13-35
(Holy Week:Easter Vigil, Saturday, or Easter Sunday)

*Suddenly, without warning, Jesus stood before them and said,
"Peace!"* Mt 28:9

Today is the day of resurrection! Today is the day of
victory over death! No matter what the struggle, no matter
what the sin, Jesus gives us all a way out! He does not leave
us condemned in sin. He does not leave us on a dead end
course to death.

Throughout the past days of Lent God has been doing a
work to reveal our sin to us. Lent calls us to see our sin, and
to have an attitude of repentance, an attitude of readiness to
change. Easter is the call to really let go of that sinful area in
our life. We do not need to go back to it.

The word for today is that of peace and deliverance. Jesus
wants to deliver us. He wants to set us free. The chains of sin
and death have been broken through his death. He bore our
sin and our sorrow. Today he rises in joy! He rises to
manifest once and for all that he has set us free. The enemy
has been conquered. Victory has come through the resurrection of Jesus Christ!

Can we possibly imagine the sheer amazement of his

followers? Imagine if Socrates rose from the dead after he was killed, or if Ghandi rose from the dead. Their followers and disciples would have been unstoppable! They would have been convinced beyond any argument of the rightness of their master's teachings.

So it was with the followers of Jesus. His crucifixion and resurrection from the dead became the central force of their entire preaching. This gave final authority to the words of Jesus. More importantly, it gave final and absolute proof of his victory over sin and death for everyone who would receive it from him.

What about us? Are we ready to receive his victory over sin and death in our life? Are we ready to let go of the sinful areas of our life God has called us to crucify during Lent? It is not enough to just repeatedly try to still them. We must also let them go. We must get on to new life. We must move on past crucifixion if we are really to be "born again." This is the central message of Easter. There is life after death. There is victory over sin and the death sin brings. This is simply a matter of receiving it and moving on. Are we ready to do that with our sinful life today? I encourage you: Just do it! Be resurrected! Be born again! Rise with Christ today! □

Part III

The Easter Season

Easter Mystery
Matthew 28:8-15 (1:Monday)

Go and carry the news. v. 10

The octave of Easter now begins to unfold. Now we begin to pass through the various accounts of the resurrection. As we shall see, the accounts vary as to specifics, but they all agree on one thing: Jesus Christ is risen from the dead. Alleluia!

It is interesting that on this central truth of Christianity, the various Gospel accounts simply do not agree. In the other parts of Jesus' life and death it is possible to harmonize the various perspectives of four Gospels . . . much like viewing the same tree from four different angles. But concerning the resurrection, there are some things that simply do not seem to agree.

Matthew says that Jesus told Mary to tell the apostles to go to Galilee to see him resurrected. Luke has his resurrection happening only in Jerusalem. John puts the two together. In the synoptics Jesus encourages them to touch him to prove that he is not a ghost. In John's Gospel Jesus tells Mary not to touch or cling to him because he had not yet ascended to the Father. Some of these things can be harmonized, but this seems artificial at best. It seems that there are, in fact, contradictory reports about the details of his resurrection.

This does not discredit the one central fact of the resurrection. Something more than extraordinary had just happened. They were "half overjoyed, half fearful." They were constantly being told not to be afraid. No doubt, they were less than rational through these Easter days. Does that mean nothing happened? No. It is precisely because something did happen, and on that they all did agree . . . Jesus rose from the dead! There can be no question about that from the Gospel accounts.

There is another mystery to unfold in these Easter octave readings. Jesus appears at different times in many different ways. Sometimes he is immediately recognizable. Sometimes he is recognized only in his words or at the blessing of the bread. Sometimes his body is touchable, with the human qualities of being able to eat, or bear the scars from crucifixion. At other times, it is supernatural, able suddenly to appear through locked doors and solid walls.

Jesus wants to surprise us this Easter. He wants to appear in a way and in a place where we may least expect him. Will we let Jesus do that this year? We have moved through Lent and Holy Week. Now it is time to move on into Easter. The way is not always predictable. It is filled with mystery and anticipation. It is filled with risk. Will you dare to walk through the Easter octave this week?   □

She Loved Much
John 20:11-18 (1:Tuesday)

"I have seen the Lord!" she announced. v. 18

Whom did Jesus appear to first? An apostle? A man? No. Jesus appeared to a woman. Did he appear to a woman of "reputation"? No. He appeared to a woman of ill repute, a converted prostitute. Today's Gospel gives us some instruction about the role of women in ministry. It also gives some challenges to men.

First, we can see that the women, not the men, remain the most faithful. Except for a traditionally teenage John, it is a woman who stands at the foot of the cross. It is women who are faithfully watching as Joseph of Arimathea and Nicodemus prepare Jesus' body for burial. The male apostles have scattered in the hour of trial. Therefore, it is appropriate that Jesus first appears to the faithful women in his resurrection.

Notice, too, that it is Mary Magdalene who first announces the good news of Jesus' resurrection from the dead. She announces the fact of the empty tomb to Simon Peter and John. Then she announces that she has "seen the Lord," and all Jesus told her, to the disciples. Jesus has brought her back from death to life in his ministry, so she owes all to Jesus and is totally unafraid to speak the truth.

There is a two-fold lesson in her relationship with the male apostles and disciples in this episode. One, she is unafraid to speak the truth. Some of the apostles, like Thomas, may doubt the resurrection, but she is fearless. Second, she works in union with the male apostles even when they are less than cooperative. She faithfully reports to them all she has seen and heard. We get an indication that she sought their authority, even when they doubted. She knew her own unique authority as a woman and was confident enough in that not to usurp theirs. She was fulfilled, confident, and unafraid.

Lastly, her response is always from the heart. She was weeping at the foot of the cross. She was weeping at the empty tomb. This was no exercise in masculine "objectivity." Her heart was in it all. The heart is the place where the New Covenant is first written, therefore, it is appropriate that Jesus would rise and appear to those who respond with their whole heart.

Do we give our heart to the crucifixion and resurrection of Jesus, or do we just walk through Holy Week and Easter as an objective historical and theological drama? Are we confident enough of our call from Christ and role in the church that we do not need to seek someone else's? These are important lessons. They are taught today not by an apostle or prophet. They are taught by a simple and penitent woman. They are lessons that say much to us! □

No Shortcuts
Luke 24:13-35 (1:Wednesday)

Two of them that same day were making their way to a village named Emmaus. v. 13

Today we have one of the most important, but most often overlooked, passages in the New Testament: the story of the two disciples on the road to Emmaus.

On Holy Thursday we celebrated the institution of the Lord's Supper, or Eucharist. Today we see it given by Christ himself in a special way. On Holy Thursday he spoke the words, "This is my body . . . this is my blood," but he stayed in their midst physically. Today he blesses the bread, is recognized, and then disappears from their physical sight! Holy Thursday is before the cross and resurrection. Today is after! On Holy Thursday Jesus is present both sacramentally and humanly. Today he is present sacramentally in the bread, even though he has humanly disappeared. Today's Gospel is a symbolic type of what is still being lived out in the Eucharist.

Notice the pattern of the Gospel. First, there is the Word, then there is the sacrament. Jesus shares the Scriptures for a full day's walk before he blesses the bread. He opens their minds. He waits until their hearts are burning! He waits further until they invite him into their house before he blesses the bread for them.

Another point should be noted. Jesus doesn't just use one particular Scripture. He goes through the entire Old Testament and points out every Scripture that refers to himself! This was a long Bible study! It took a whole day for the "Liturgy of the Word" before they were really ready for the "Liturgy of the Eucharist."

Do we give Jesus that kind of time with our use of Scripture? Are we willing to walk with him a full day before we receive the sacraments? Are we willing to listen to him teach us the lessons of Scripture? This is a lesson we Catholics need to rediscover.

There is a lesson for Protestants as well. Jesus wasn't really seen until the blessing of the bread. Even though he taught Scripture in a way that made the two disciples' hearts burn within, they didn't recognize him until he blessed the bread.

Do we sometimes limit the revelation of Jesus to the teaching of Scripture? Are we willing to go beyond his partial revelation in the Word to his complete revelation in the sacrament? Have our eyes really been opened to the full recognition of Jesus? Today we see the need for Word and sacrament. Be we Catholic or Protestant, we all need to walk the full Emmaus walk with Jesus. Any shortcuts only cut us short of Jesus' full revelation in our own lives.   □

Focus on Jesus
Luke 24:35-48 (1:Thursday)

Why are you disturbed? Why do such ideas cross your mind? v.38

We too are sometimes confused about the resurrection and our faith in Christ. We praise, but we are also afraid. Sometimes all of it seems too unreal and we lose faith. Sometimes it all seems overwhelmingly real and we lose courage. We shrink in fright before the awesome power of God. Today the Lord calls us to clear our mind and focus back on the simple gospel of Jesus.

Jesus does something that puts the apostles into bedlam today. He suddenly appears in the room with them, out of nowhere! No entrance at all. Just presence. This is enough to unnerve even the most faithful of followers, much less this motley crew that just days before had abandoned and denied him. They were scared to death.

Jesus puts them at ease. He wishes them peace. He allows them to observe that he is still flesh and blood. Despite the supernatural resurrection, he is the same Jesus they always knew. He is still human. To prove it, he asks for food and eats with them. This is always a sign of friendship and peace. Then Jesus begins to teach them again, just as before. All is restored. They are forgiven. They are still his friends, his disciples, indeed even his apostles.

Jesus then gives another promise. They are to carry on his mission to preach to all the nations on earth, but they are not yet ready. Their training is still not complete, even after these resurrectional appearances and instructions. They must be clothed with the power of the Spirit. This will come later at Pentecost. Until then they are to simply be patient and wait.

What about us? Do we wait for the power of the Spirit before we try to tell the good news? Do we sometimes find our mind troubled and confused about Jesus? Let him calm you. Let him eat supper with you. Let him teach you. Then your mind will clear, you will be empowered by the Spirit, and you will know what to say when the time comes.

We are given a great commission in today's Gospel. Like the apostles we are frail, fragile, and human. Like the apostles we are confused and afraid. Jesus can calm us, teach us, and empower us. Then, like the apostles, we will also go forth to be his witnesses to all the earth! Do not be afraid. Center your thoughts on Jesus. Then all doubts and confusions will disappear. □

Our First Love
John 21:1-14 (1:Friday)

Later, at the sea of Tiberias, Jesus showed himself to the disciples [once again]. v. 1

Jesus is calling us back to our first love in the Gospel today. So much has happened since our initial conversion to Christ. It has become so complicated. Sin has muddied the water again. In the beginning, following Jesus was so simple and clear. It was life or death. Now things seem unclear again. We get confused. Today Jesus calls us back to our first love.

Peter finds himself in the same situation today. So much has happened since his first conversion to follow Jesus. It became complicated. It was complicated by the religion of the Jews. It was complicated by the politics of Israel and Rome. It was complicated by the crucifixion of Jesus and his own denial of Christ. What started out so simple had become a complicated affair indeed!

Today Jesus calls Peter and the other disciples back to the innocence of their first love and conversion when they became his followers. How?

Notice that this scene takes place in Galilee rather than Jerusalem. This is the place where they first followed him. Furthermore, he works a miracle that is almost identical to the miracle that won Peter in the first place. How could this not win Peter's heart again? More importantly, how could it not restore his heart to that first innocence and joy of his conversion? Today Jesus is taking Peter back to the beginning . . . right back to where it all started for him.

Before we get too excited about returning to this seemingly trouble free state of grace in Christ, we should remember the experience of Peter and the others after Pentecost. They were imprisoned. Yet, they were jailed willingly and with joy. They no longer ran away and denied Christ.

Are we willing to do the same? We can only do so if we allow Jesus to take us back to our first love for him. What was it like before and after we first followed Christ? Why did we first follow him? Why did we first become members of the church or of a particular community? Remembering these important decisions of the past helps to put the present into perspective. It helps us to return to our first love, Jesus Christ. □

Spread the Word in Firm Belief
Mark 16:9-15 (1:Saturday)

When they heard that he was alive... they refused to believe it. v. 11

Mark's account continues to expose even the most embarrassingly human aspects of Jesus' followers. Mark is extremely candid about Jesus' rebukes of the apostles for their lack of beliefs, petty differences, and pointless arguments. At times, Jesus appears an exasperated leader of a bunch of childish, immature clowns. Today even after the resurrection, the situation has not really changed.

Mark's words are pointed and brief. Today he covers two stories in one, both the Mary Magdalene and Road to Emmaus accounts of the resurrection. He includes two important points discretely omitted by the other Gospels. The apostles refuse to believe either Mary or the two disciples from the road to Emmaus! It takes a personal visit from Jesus and their own personal experience to convince the others.

Mark's account doesn't portray a Jesus who wishes them all peace and forgiveness. Jesus rebukes them for their lack of faith and closed-minded stubbornness. Yes, he is again at table with them, but is quite frank about his displeasure with their continual worldly attitudes.

Notice that he is not just upset about their lack of faith in him. He is upset about their lack of faith in those sent by him after the resurrection. This is not just a matter of personal faith in Jesus. This is a matter of faith in the Jesus who works corporately through the church and Christian community.

Once he has corrected their mistakes, Jesus is quick to announce the good news. Despite their human sinfulness, he gives them the great commission: "Go into the whole world and proclaim the good news to all creation" (Mk 16:15). This is not only for the apostles as in the other Gospels. It is for all believers!

No doubt, we too have experienced a doubtful response when we share the good news of Jesus Christ with others. Sometimes we also doubt when someone shares a story about some supernatural occurrence attributed to Jesus. We expect others to believe us, but are we sometimes slow to believe another's account of Jesus, or must we see it for ourselves?

Today Jesus rebukes us for our unbelief, but do not despair. He implies that once we overcome this failure, we will be ready to evangelize others. We cannot expect people to receive until we have received. We cannot expect from others what we do not do ourselves. First learn, then teach. First believe. Then spread the faith!   □

Extraordinarily Ordinary
John 20:19-31 (1:Second Sunday)

Receive the Holy Spirit. . . . Do not persist in your unbelief, but believe! vv. 22, 27

Today's Gospel does two things: It sets the apostles apart for leadership, and it points out that they are just like you and me. They are common and uncommon; ordinary and extraordinary. This is part of the mystery of the church.

First, they are given a special place of leadership among the believers. Jesus breathes the Holy Spirit on them even before the general outpouring and empowerment at Pentecost. They are given an extraordinary outpouring of the Spirit, an extra help, so that their role of leadership would be especially anointed.

On the other hand, the apostles are also very ordinary. They are like you and me. Thomas refuses to believe. None of them believed earlier in other accounts, now it is Thomas' turn. He has to actually put his fingers into Jesus' wounds before he will believe. Part of this is good, he is not easily deceived. But part of this is bad. Jesus rebuked the others for their failure to believe, and today he almost does the same with Thomas: "Do not persist in your unbelief." The tone is not gentle. It is stern.

We too are sometimes doubtful of the work of the resurrected Christ in our midst. It is all a bit too supernatural for us. It is too extraordinary. We need something a bit more ordinary and understandable before we will believe. While this can be a good, built-in part of our character to "discern the spirits" of supernatural occurrences, it can also be bad. It can cause us to be less than cooperative with the supernatural work of God in our lives.

Ironically, we also sometimes fail to see the supernatural mystery in the leadership of the church. We do not see the successors to the apostles. We just see sinners. Today's Gospel calls us to look further and see the special anointing of the Spirit even upon the very ordinary and human leaders in the church. This is a matter of forgiveness and tolerance. After all, we too have sinned from time to time. They are just as human as you and me.

How do we handle the mystery of the supernatural in the midst of the natural? We are called to go beyond the natural to the extraordinary and supernatural. We are also to be comforted by the ever-present ordinariness of the natural. To be at peace in the resurrected Christ, we must learn to see both and live in the creative tension between the two. This is part of the mystery of Christ and the church. □

Go to the Source
John 3:1-8 (2:Monday)

Flesh begets flesh, Spirit begets spirit. v. 6

Today we have Nicodemus approaching Jesus. He is at a conversion point. He says that Jesus must be a teacher come from God, or else he could not perform the signs and wonders he does. Jesus gives a reply that is both negative and positive. It is mystery. What is the answer?

Jesus gives Nicodemus that now classical Scripture—you must be born again. He emphasizes that this must be a rebirth of the spirit. He does include the rite of baptism, which was used by the itinerate preachers of his day, as a sign of this renewal.

The negative side to this is that Jesus is saying that signs and wonders are not enough. Nicodemus had equated Jesus being a teacher from God with his accompanying signs and wonders. Though he does elsewhere, Jesus never responds to this question in his conversation with Nicodemus. He immediately calls Nicodemus deeper. He calls him to the invisible things of the Spirit. These things are beyond externals. They are like the wind.

On the positive side, Jesus is encouraging Nicodemus in the dialogue. He is not being rebuked. He is being called. Nicodemus is still on the outside looking in, but at least he is looking! God's grace is touching the life of this Pharisee with a new spark of renewal. Jesus is fanning the spark into full flame.

The flame did burn in Nicodemus' heart for the passion. We see that when all the apostles, save John, desert Jesus; Nicodemus and Joseph of Arimathea stand by him at his trial, crucifixion, and burial. Tradition has it they both became disciples of Jesus in the early church. Grace was beginning to work in Nicodemus' life. Jesus knew it.

Do we limit God's grace to signs and wonders? These "signs and wonders" can be any external aspect of the

Christian life or life in community we find exciting. Still we must have the Spirit given to the church. We must have the charism of the participating community to which we belong. We can do all the externals well and never know the Spirit and the charism. If we have the Spirit, however, we will do all the externals better.

Let Jesus call you past the signs of the Spirit to himself. Let him take you past the stream, to the well. Let him take you to the source. Otherwise, you may not be experiencing the real kingdom of God at all. □

Windows and Pillars
John 3:7-15 (2:Tuesday)

You hold the office of teacher of Israel and still you do not understand these matters? v. 10

Today I would like to focus on two aspects of the church: the succession of the apostles and the succession of saints. Apostolic succession was understood by the early church as a structural, traceable succession of appointed, elected, and ordained leaders or bishops, back to the apostles themselves. The succession of the saints is a matter of the wind of the Spirit that cannot be traced at all. It can raise up a saint from clergy or laity, male or female, educated or uneducated. It knows no limitations concerning one's external state of life.

Jesus' words yesterday to Nicodemus had both a positive and negative tone. They are critical. They are an astonished indictment against the ignorance of the "clergy" of Jesus' time. They accuse the *magisterium* of his day of a worldly and carnal perspective that can only be properly viewed from a spiritual perspective.

Sometimes, we too see a conflict between the saints and the magisterium or teaching authority of the church. Sometimes those raised up by the Spirit outside the normal structures of the church have great difficulty in obtaining the support or cooperation of the official church. Historically, the saints were often resisted and even brought to trial and condemned in the church before they were vindicated and canonized. Today or tomorrow will be no exception.

We need to also recognize that the Spirit works through the official church. The Spirit was breathed onto the apostles in a special way after the resurrection, as well as poured out on all believers, including the apostles. The early church held apostolic succession as their guarantee of correct teaching in the Christian community. Therefore, to say that the Spirit is not at work in the succession of the apostles through the bishops and magisterium of the church would be incomplete and untrue.

How do we view the succession of the apostles and the succession of the saints today? Do we limit the work of the Spirit to one or the other? If we do, we are not really "catholic" or "full." The house of God needs structure. But any good house has lots of windows to let in the wind.   □

Love Freely
John 3:16-21 (2:Wednesday)

God so loved the world that he gave his only Son, that whoever believes in him may not die but may have eternal life. v. 16

Today we reflect on the classic Scripture for salvation in and through Jesus Christ. Out of this classic Scripture, there are two words that say it all: "loved" and "gave."

The whole point of the incarnation is love. Jesus came forth from love in order to love. He came to love so that others might love. This is the whole point of Christianity.

This is not a love as is known and practiced in the world. The word "love" is essentially connected to the other word: "gave." To love and to give are inseparably bound together.

If you really love, you must also give.

The world's love agrees with this only to a point. The world loves only so it might be loved. It gives in order to receive. Ultimately this is a selfish love. It is not really giving. It is simply investing.

Jesus' love is radically different. It gives without expecting anything in return. It loves simply for love's sake. The irony of the gospel of Jesus is that when you love and give in this way, you get more back from God than another human being could possibly give.

This also frees human love to be fully operative again. When you love another person expecting to be loved in return, you end up choking the love out of this relationship through possessiveness. When you let go of the person you love, then your love is freed from the sin of possessiveness and the other person is freed to love you in return as an act of their own free will, rather than as an act of compulsion and guilt. In this the relationship moves into the real freedom and more solidly based commitments of Christian love.

Do we really love with the love of Christ, or are we still expecting something in return? Do we love God for love's sake, or in order to gain salvation? Do we love people the same way? This is not love. It is only selfish investment. Love God and you gain eternal life as a free gift from God. Love people and you gain healthy relationships. Try to possess or command people or God and you end up with nothing. Choose love and gain real life.   □

Say "Yes" to the Spirit
John 3:31-36 (2:Thursday)

He does not ration his gift of the Spirit. v. 34

Jesus tells us that he has come that we might have life and have it abundantly! He does not desire that any of us lives only a part of the full potential he gives us. He gives his full self to all of his followers! We do not get only a part of Jesus when we fully give our life to him. At the same time, we are only one part of the body of Christ. No one of us has it all.

This is especially true in the area of the gifts of the Spirit. The general gift of the Spirit is never rationed or parcelled out. But the particular gifts of the Spirit are given to each according to the particular will of God. This means two things are true: All of us are given gifts, but most of us do not possess them all. Two abuses are also prevalent: Being closed to accepting the gifts of the Spirit, or claiming to possess more gifts than God has really given. Pride is usually the sin in both cases. The inverted pride of false humility is the first. The overt pride of egotism in the second. We should be humble enough to be open to whatever gifts God wants to give us, and poor enough in spirit to do our part in accepting the gift when it is given.

There are two traditional lists of the gifts of the Spirit: Paul's list in 1 Corinthians 12-14, and Isaiah's in Isaiah 11. Paul's list is more external for use in ministry. Isaiah's list is more internal, not unlike what Paul would call the "fruit of the Spirit" in his letter to the Galatians. One is corporate, the other is more personal. One is more exclusive, the other more inclusive. We may rightly only be given one or a few of Paul's list. But we may rightly open ourselves to all of Isaiah's list of wisdom, understanding, counsel, strength, knowledge, fear of the Lord, and delight in the Lord.

In these latter gifts we are again reminded that the general gift of the Spirit of God is given fully to every follower of Jesus who desires it. It will not necessarily make you a charismatic superstar. It will make you a saint. Sainthood is a vocation to which we are all called. It is a gift to all. The question is, will you accept it?

It is like accepting a gift here on earth from people. When a person hands you a gift, you must reach back actively and consciously if you are to receive it. The same is generally true with God. We must be open to the gift of the Spirit and learn to cultivate those gifts if we are to see them be fruitful in our lives.

Are we really open to God's gifts? Will we take the time to cultivate the gifts we already have? Are we interested in the gifts for ourselves or for the good of others and the glory of God? Finally, are we interested in becoming a charismatic show, or do we want to become a saint? Be a saint first and the other will follow. Be totally open to the Spirit and the gifts will take care of themselves. □

The Highest Law
John 6:1-15 (2:Friday)

A vast crowd kept following him . . . Jesus then went up the mountain. vv. 2-3

How do we respond to an intrusion? In a burn-out conscious society, it is easy to overcompensate in the other direction. Within the church this can easily degenerate from an attitude emphasizing selfless service to an attitude of self-serving. This happens when the average church or community worker begins emphasizing his or her solitude or prayer time so much, they actually quit serving others properly. This means they serve only themselves. This means they actually stop serving God. Granted, we all need our contemplation to balance our action, but contemplation can easily degenerate into an excuse for selfishness.

Today's Gospel gives us the challenge to balance the two in love. First, we see that Jesus has actually pulled away to the mountain with his disciples to avoid the crowd. This was, no doubt, an attempt to get some quality time both with God and with his serious followers. It was a time of retreat.

The crowd intruded upon his privacy. They found him

out and came to him in droves. How does he respond to them? Does he tell them he is "in a meeting"? No, he does not. He sees their genuine need. He sees that he is, in fact, able to help them. So he ministers to the multitude.

What is the result of this selfless service? The disciples actually gather up more food than they gave out! Not only did a miracle occur by his increasing the loaves and fishes to feed the vast multitude, another miracle occurred that the disciples actually received back more than they gave. Because they were willing to give away the little they thought they had, they received back even more in return.

What about us? Are we really willing to take the risk of service, even when it is inconvenient? Are we willing to disrupt our prayer when real charity demands? I am not suggesting doing away with the real discipline or contemplation. I am only suggesting that love be our highest discipline and law. This was, after all, the practice of the great Christian hermits of history. This is often overlooked in a society that feeds the self-serving deception of "Looking out for number one." This philosophy does not essentially integrate with real Christianity.   □

Sacrificial Solitude
John 6:16-21 (2:Saturday)

They sighted Jesus approaching the boat, walking on the water.
v. 19

Despite Jesus' availability to the disruption of his solitude in yesterday's Gospel, he still went back into the solitude of the mountain after the miraculous ministry to the multitudes. After the miracle, the crowds wanted to make him a king, but since this was not the purpose of his ministry, he escaped into solitude once more. There he stayed, even to the point of missing the departure with his disciples towards their Capernaum ministry based on the other side of the lake.

Jesus' availability for the disruptions of spontaneous ministry did not mean that he did not take pains to enter into solitude. As we can see from today's Gospel, he did this even to the point of missing an "appointment." In today's Gospel he literally "missed the boat" in order to pray! He knew where his real priorities were. He knew that solitude and prayer were vitally important.

It is not unlike what was said of St. Francis of Assisi over one thousand years later. It is said that when Francis was disrupted during prayer to minister, that he would always go back to prayer. He did this even if it meant staying up extra hours at night or rising a few hours earlier in the morning. Notice this is not selfish contemplation. It is sacrificial. It is out of love for God that he gave God the time he wanted for his appointment.

What is the result of this prayer priority? It would seem that this lack of sleep would burn you out more. It would seem that missing appointments, or even travel connections, would create even more stress.

This is not the case with Jesus. This prayer priority gave Jesus the strength and created the opportunity for him to walk on the water. If you want to see your ministry become miraculous in its spiritual power, you have to give priority to prayer. It must also be a selfless exercise for God. Furthermore, it often defies the cool human logic of a schedule or a technique.

Do we give God time? Are we willing to be interrupted at prayer for charity, and then make up the prayer time through sacrifice? If we are not, then our contemplation is not really like Christ, or Christian. If we are, then we will begin to see real power in both our prayer and our ministry. We will begin to "walk on the water." □

Rooted in Jesus
John 6:22-29 (3:Monday)

This is the work of God: have faith in the One whom he sent. v. 29

Today we are cautioned against two common forms of idolatry: sign seeking, and workaholism. We have already spoken about the dangers of sign seeking. Signs and wonders are gifts from God. They are, in fact, promised to the followers of Jesus. They were performed by Jesus himself, but they are not Jesus. They are not God. We should seek the Giver, not the gifts.

Of course, in today's Gospel Jesus says they are not seeking him because he performed signs and wonders, but because they had eaten their fill of the loaves. This is moving beyond mere signs and wonders. This is a sign and wonder that has direct and tangible effects on lives: feeding the hungry.

In today's Christian communities, many people clamor after signs and wonders. But they can easily be abused and degenerate into spectacles that create religious fanatics rather than authentically radical (or rooted) followers of Jesus Christ. We must remember that Jesus' miracles had a directly tangible result in a needy person's life: healing the sick, feeding the hungry, or raising the dead. They were acts of love. They were acts of mercy.

This has direct relevance to our works of mercy as well. As a reaction against abused signs and wonders, some will dig into corporate works of mercy in an attempt to be a more "authentic" Christian. No doubt, corporate works of mercy are important. Jesus tells us we will be judged according to the mercy we have shown others. I, myself, am an honorary chairperson for a relief and development agency called Mercy Corps International. But many times we can become workaholics for Christ and miss Christ himself. We can also become self-righteous as we snobbishly look down on the more charismatic followers of Christ. We must center on Jesus and Jesus alone. Then our works of mercy will really do the work of God. Then they will also include the miraculous.

Do we sometimes seek the gifts and miss the Giver? Do we get stuck in signs and wonders and miss the Wonderful Counselor? Do we perform works of mercy and miss the Merciful One? If we simply have faith in Jesus we will find signs and wonders very present in our life and our ministry of mercy much more effective. Seek faith, hope, and love. These are the greatest gifts. These all come from simple faith in Jesus. □

The Bread of Life
John 6:30-35 (3:Tuesday)

I myself am the bread of life. v. 35

There are two different contemporary schools of thought concerning this Scripture. One is sacramental. The other is nonsacramental. By and large, one is Catholic, the other is held by many Christians of other traditions. However, integrated theologians from both traditions are beginning to see truth in one another's perspective. Let us try to do the same.

The nonsacramental school sees this as referring to Jesus in general. The prophets of old are said to actually eat God's word before speaking it. Later, in John 6, Jesus will again say that the flesh only begets flesh, while spirit begets spirit, and that it is his words that are spirit and life. Jesus is seen as the living Word. Therefore, it is not inappropriate to speak of the "bread of the word."

This school also sees this Scripture as an analogy. We know that Jesus used many analogies and parables. He even calls himself a "shepherd." But was Jesus really a shepherd? He also calls himself a "door." But is Jesus a physical door? Do we make sacraments of these analogies? Here, they say,

Jesus calls himself the bread of life by way of analogy to emphasize that he is our spiritual food and drink, our only real nourishment.

Catholics believe there is something more to consider: The response of the crowd. The other analogies draw the crowds closer to Jesus. This one repels them. They all desert him after this discourse. Jesus even has to ask the apostles if they are going to leave him too. In essence, they say that they have nowhere else to go after already following him this far. Obviously, something was up. This was more than a simple analogy.

The early church saw this Scripture sacramentally in light of the other Eucharistic Scriptures; they easily connected this analogy to the Eucharist and interpreted it in a sacramental way. It was of central importance to orthodox Christians in the early church. Did they fully understand this mystery? No they did not! They only knew Jesus said it, so they believed it by faith.

St. Francis said that with the eyes of the flesh we can only see bread and wine, but with the eyes of the Spirit and faith we can look further and see the Body and Blood of Jesus Christ.

But it doesn't stop here. With the eyes of flesh, we only see the mundane realities in our world. But with the eyes of faith, we can see Jesus in the people of the church and the whole human family. We can see Jesus in our world! This view sacramentalizes the church and the whole world in Jesus who is himself the sacrament sent to redeem the whole world. Of course, the issue is: *Will we receive him?*

Are we open to the Bread of Life as he comes to us in all these ways? Do we believe he abides in us through the sacraments? Or do we accept a desacramentalized church and world? Do we only see Jesus in the sacraments without letting him break through to all areas of our life? Let Jesus break through. Let him be your bread always. Let him feed you as no one else can. □

An Open Door
John 6:35-40 (3:Wednesday)

No one who comes to me will I ever reject. v. 37

The world is a hurt place, a place filled with rejection—rejection by parents, by friends, by co-workers. This rejection causes pain, which leads to anger and death. Sometimes we are all too willing to blame someone else; a parent or family member for our own sin. Their sin is not the issue. Our response is the issue at hand. Today Jesus gives us a way back from death to life, from anger to love, and from rejection to acceptance. He never rejects anyone who sincerely seeks him.

I remember the saying, "If God seems far away, who moved?" God never moves away from us. He is always close by. If he seems far away, it is usually because we have moved away from him through sin. St. James says to sinners, "Draw close to God and he will draw close to you."

Sin, even habitual small sins, take the edge off of our spiritual life and eventually even break our full communion with God if left unchecked. God offers us a way back through repentance and forgiveness if we are sincere in our conversion.

A word of warning here: Sirach warns us about presuming on forgiveness through an insincere repentance. This means we give ourself license to sin for a season because we know that forgiveness will be given later. Under these conditions forgiveness is not given until repentance is real. This means renouncing sin with the intention to never sin again. If we do sin, forgiveness is again given if repentance is sincere.

The same is true between people. Abbot Aelred of Rievaulx is said to have never asked any professed monk to leave his monastery. He always gave an offender a choice to repent. If he left, it was essentially because he chose to. This does not mean leadership may not have had to help him to see the choice he made through his actions. But in the end, the individual actually made the choice.

What about us? Do we allow Jesus to heal us of our sense of rejection? Do we return to him when given the choice? Do we do this sincerely, or are we toying with God's forgiveness? Lastly, do we reject each other in community, or do we offer God's forgiveness?

Jesus stands before us today as an open door. All we need do is turn around and walk through if we want to be accepted by God, the church, and the community again. □

Accept Forgiveness
John 6:41-51 (3:Thursday)

No one can come to me unless the Father who sent me draws him. v. 44

You hear many people complain today that they want the Spirit to work in their lives, but they are sure they are not worthy of such a gift. Today's Gospel blows a gaping hole in that whole way of thinking. It gives you an assurance that God is already at work in your life.

When Simon Peter confesses his faith in Christ, saying, "You are the Messiah, the Son of the living God," Jesus assures him: "Blest are you, Simon son of John! No mere man has revealed this to you, but my heavenly Father" (Mt 16:17). In a similar vein, St. Paul says, "It is God who, in his good will toward you, begets in you any measure of desire or achievement" (Phil 2:13).

What does this mean? If you even desire for God to work in your life, he already is! If you even desire to follow Jesus, you have already begun! If you even desire the gift of the Holy Spirit, you are already receiving the gift! This is good news! No one is beyond grace. If you even desire grace, you are already being given grace. Yes, you might have more to do to grow in that grace, but the work of grace has already begun in your life.

Some people think their sins are somehow unforgiveable. Jesus does say that the sin against the Holy Spirit is unforgiveable. What does this mean? Hebrews says, "For when men have once been enlightened and have tasted the heavenly gift and become sharers in the Holy Spirit, . . . and then have fallen away, it is *impossible to make them repent again*" (Heb 6:4, 6).

Those who have really committed the "unforgiveable sin" are so hardened that they do not even want to repent. They couldn't be made to repent. If you even desire to repent, that is proof that you haven't committed the unforgiveable sin. The only sin you are guilty of is pride: thinking that you are so extraordinary that you cannot even sin ordinarily. Guess what? You are just like everyone else! Your sin is really quite ordinary. It is also quite forgiveable.

Are you assured of God working in your life today? If you have even the faintest desire to serve him, then God is already at work. If you have even a remote desire to repent of any sin, that sin is forgiveable. Do not let yourself get depressed or dejected. Do not let the devil lie to you. Do not give in to subtle pride. Just accept God's ordinary forgiveness and cooperate with God's ordinary grace. □

Receive the Body of Jesus
John 6:52-59 (3:Friday)

If you do not eat the flesh of the Son of Man and drink his blood, you have no life in you. v. 53

Many of us can go to daily Communion and still not really be eating of his Flesh and Blood in a life-changing way. Receiving Communion is the greatest "altar call" in sacrament. How sad that so many come forward without really seeing or hearing Jesus. We Catholics have tended to sacramentalize the notion of eating and drinking of the Body and Blood of Jesus so that we overlook doing this in a way that permeates our whole way of life. It must be admitted that the eating and drinking his Body and Blood for the sake of conversion and personal transformation is probably more what Jesus had in mind with his disciples.

It must also be remembered that this emphasis has been constantly and officially taught by the Catholic church. It has been constantly lived by the saints. But it hasn't always been lived and preached that way by individual Catholics, both clergy and laity.

Also, one must realize that the blessings and graces of the Sacrament of the Eucharist cannot be found fully outside of the Catholic church. Yes, you may find particular pastors, bishops, and churches that share in greater or lesser degrees with the Catholic teaching of Eucharist and even share in the concept of transubstantiation. Yet the "common union" or "communion" that both symbolizes and causes a full unity in the structural body, doctrinal mind, and charismatic spirit of the body of Christ going back in time through the succession of the apostles to Jesus himself, can be found nowhere else. Only Catholic Christians possess this full unity and universally share in it. This does not mean that other Christians are not saved. It does not mean that Catholics are better than all other Christians. It only means that we possess a gift of God that cannot be found anywhere else. Unless you receive the Body and Blood of Christ in the Eucharist as a Catholic Christian, you cannot fully possess this particular gift of life in Christ.

Are we willing to open ourselves to fully eating and drinking the Body and Blood of Jesus Christ today? Let us really receive him in a way that permeates our whole day. Let us receive him in a way that fully unifies the body of Christ with integrity. This is a tall order indeed! We may never see it in our lifetime as we work towards Christian unity, but we can do our part. We can begin with ourselves. Then we can reach out to others. Receive Jesus' Body and Blood today. ☐

To Whom Else Can We Go?
John 6:60-69 (3:Saturday)

Do you want to leave me too? v. 67

The results of Jesus' discourse on the Bread of Life were not good. The text has it that, "From this time on, many of his disciples broke away and would not remain in his company any longer." As we said earlier; this was understood as more than a parable or analogy. It was meant literally. This was a reality many of his disciples were not prepared to accept.

The same is true in today's Christian churches. When confronted with the central position of the Eucharist in the worship of the early church, many modern congregations would rather hang on to their Western novelty and independence than really conform to the apostolic tradition of the early church. We of the modern West are noted for talking about being like the early church. When that requires a real rethinking and change in our attitude and practice towards something like Eucharist, however, we choose to remain as we are. In short, we also "break away" from the company of Jesus as he was worshiped and preached by the early church of authentic apostolic origins.

The same holds true for us of the Catholic Christian faith. Sometimes Jesus gives us hard sayings. Sometimes they seem more than we can handle. In order to really eat his Flesh and drink his Blood, we must be willing to hear his Word and imitate his flesh and blood life while he was here on earth. This means radical change in many areas of our lifestyles with which we have grown quite comfortable. This means sacrifice. The saints have done this before us. Often-times, though, we find out we don't really want to be saints. We just want to get by. In this we also break away from the lifestyle and faith of the apostles who accompanied Jesus.

The apostles didn't fully understand these Eucharistic words of Jesus. Neither will we always understand. But like the apostles, we can still be faithful. They said, "Lord, to whom else can we go? You have the words of everlasting life." Sometimes this is all we can hang on to. We won't always understand, but we can be faithful.

Will we be faithful today? We do not always understand exactly how to eat the Flesh and drink the Blood of Christ. But we can at least be open and try. This may involve liturgy, sacraments, and worship. It may involve lifestyle. Either way, our life is to become a sacrament. Our life is to become a thanksgiving, a "Eucharist." Then will we not only receive the Body and Blood of Christ, we will distribute him to others.   □

Fleecing the Flock
John 10:11-18 (4:Monday)

I am the good shepherd; the good shepherd lays down his life for the sheep. v. 11

How different are the hired hands of today's Gospel! When they see a wolf attacking, they turn the other way and run! Why? They are not really shepherds, nor have they personally invested in the sheep. They are just doing a job.

These hirelings are much like many of the professional pastors of today's churches. For them it is only a job, or an entrepreneur's opportunity at best. They are more than willing to offer their services in exchange for the security of a comfortable way of life. As soon as that security is threatened, they are quick to seek another flock to fleece.

This is especially true in the mega-church phenomenon. These pastors often live a luxuriously affluent lifestyle. Their mega church provides them with a mega home and a mega car. They grow very accustomed to a mega lifestyle. If this materialistic way of life is threatened, or if they find opportunity to climb yet higher on the economic ladder, they are off to yet another "ministry." It is these charleton approaches which have put such a bad taste in the mouths of so many people towards legitimate ministries.

Paul talks of a similar phenomenon in his day. He says, "Such men value religion only as a means of personal gain" (1 Tm 6:5). Or again, "There will be terrible times in the last days. Men will be lovers of self and of money, . . . lovers of pleasure rather than of God as they make a pretense of religion but negate its power" (2 Tm 3:1-5). Such a description could easily fit the "hirelings" of our own religious superstars!

Jesus tells us the real Christian leader must be willing to "Lay down his life for the sheep." He will sacrifice his own wealth for the sake of others, his own gain for the gain of others. He will seek the benefits and prosperity of the sheep of the flock he shepherds rather than his own.

Of course, Jesus is the only one who is the perfect good shepherd. All the rest are still learning the way. Jesus is the teacher. Any shepherd who is following another way is no longer learning from Jesus.

Are our pastors really learning the way of the Good Shepherd? Are our churches pastored by shepherds or hirelings? If by hirelings, then we must seriously rethink the authenticity of the Christianity to which we adhere. Let us belong to the real flock, guided by real shepherds, who follow the way of the Good Shepherd. Anything other than this is false religion. □

The Devil's Deceit
John 10:22-30 (4:Tuesday)

You refuse to believe because you are not my sheep. v. 26

What is it within that makes us want to believe in Jesus? Is it the creature seeking the Creator? Is it something more? Is it logic, or is it something beyond logic? Why do we believe?

On one level it is true that our own human createdness causes us to seek the divine Creator. St. Augustine said his heart is restless until it rests in God. It has been said that there is an empty place within the human soul that can only be filled with God. When the human soul hears God's word it "knows" that the word is truth by the witness given within. Created in the image of God, there is something inherent in our humanness that causes us to recognize God.

On a similar level there is something quite logical about belief in God and Jesus. Some theologians would say that understanding leads to belief. Others would say that belief leads to understanding. Actually, both are true. Logic leads to faith in God and Christ, and faith in God and Jesus Christ makes all things logical. All creation logically leads to the Triune and Incarnate God, and the Triune and Incarnate God gives logic and completeness to all creation.

This is not the whole story. If it were, then the whole

human race would believe. As it is, only a small percentage of people do. Also, even the religious of Jesus' day did not believe in his words. Why?

Jesus says there is another spiritual reality going on that has confused things. The devil has entered the world. He tempted us to sin, and once we sin we give him even more place in our soul. He lies. He comes as light or as God, but he is not. Therefore, even philosophers and theologians can be deceived by him. By repeatedly giving in to him, he gains control of our soul and becomes our father.

Only the Spirit can clear away this confusion. Jesus forgives us our sin and gives the Spirit to all who really seek divine truth. It is the Spirit who writes the truth on our heart and soul. Therefore, it is the Spirit who enables us to bear witness to the truth of Christ and believe. If we really desire truth, Jesus will do this for us. Once this initial gift is given, it is our responsibility to respond properly. We can cause the gift to grow like a seed that grows into a fruitful vine, or we can reject it altogether and end up with the devil again.

Do we really hear the words of Christ? Does our soul resonate with his truth? If not, why? Do we really want the truth of Jesus, or will we only accept Christ on our own terms? If so, it is because we are still of the father of lies, the devil.

Accept Jesus on his own terms. Let the Spirit operate fully in your life. Then you will find that empty place inside your soul filled with God. Then will all creation begin to make sense for you again. □

Confident Humility
John 12:44-50 (4:Wednesday)

Whoever puts faith in me believes not so much in me as in him who sent me. v. 44

What a strange combination of humility and confidence! On one level he says he will not judge anyone for not following him. On another level he says that all that do not follow him will be judged by the words he proclaimed.

We too are called to such a combination of humility and confidence in Christ. We have been given the Spirit who guides us unto all truth and inspires us to proclaim the good news. We have been given the apostolic tradition through the church; and the written account of that tradition through the Scriptures. We can be confident, but we must remain humble.

This is seen in light of a proper understanding of humility. It has been said that humility is just the truth. What is the truth?

On one level we are totally and utterly dependent on God. We are absolutely nothing without him. He created us in his image, he restores that image by redeeming us from our sins through Jesus Christ. Without God, neither life nor redemption are possible. This should stir a real humility within us.

But we also have a confidence. Our life reflects something extraordinarily good. It reflects God! It was so valuable that when we lost that image by covering it up through the dirt of sin, Jesus Christ shed his own blood to cleanse us of the dirt of sin so we might fully reflect God once more. We are so valuable that Jesus died on a cross in order to save us!

Furthermore, we recognize the same goodness in others in both the church and the world. With this confidence and humility born of truth, we recognize our interdependence with one another. All creation bears God's traces, all humankind his image. So we are valuable, each according to his place in the world and the church.

Furthermore, no one of us is truly complete without the other. Especially in the church we are, as St.Paul says, "The body of Christ." Each member is unique and important. But no member of the body is independent of another. We are interdependent.

We must avoid two errors: independence and co-dependence. Independence denies its utter dependence on God and its interdependence with others. Dependence or codependence denies the real value of the human self through a low self-image and becomes overly dependent on another for a sense of self worth. Both errors lead to a dysfunctional life of pain, sadness, and death. Be utterly dependent on God and God alone. Then be healthfully interdependent with others. Then, like Jesus, we will be both confident and humble.

I would add a word of caution here about the current "dysfunctional fad." It seems that suddenly everyone is dysfunctional. Nowadays, our problem is not really our problem anymore. My mother did it to me. My father is at fault. My brothers and sisters are the real sinners. And so on. This faddish use of the word "dysfunction" is just a subtle way for New Age self-indulgence to creep in to Christianity. It gets our eyes off of Jesus and habitually onto our faults and the faults of others.

Classical dysfunctionalism refers to a diagnosed clinical psychosis that is passed on from one generation to the next. As one Christian psychologist recently said; most of us get piano lessons and play sports, most of us go to school, grow up and marry, and support ourselves and our family through employment. Mommy and Daddy may have yelled at us, or even hit us from time to time, but that doesn't mean we are "dysfunctional." We are functioning! We just need a little healing. Mommy and Daddy may have made some mistakes, but they didn't "abuse" us. The problem is not really dysfunctionalism. The problem is sin. The answer is Jesus. Trying to call it something else is often just an attempt to escape the real healing by blaming someone else for our own sinful responses. □

In or Out?
John 13:16-20 (4:Thursday)

No slave is greater than his master; no messenger outranks the one who sent him. v. 16

Do we really want to follow Jesus? Many people try to construe Jesus into a kind of New Age guru. They conform Jesus to their image of what they want out of a Saviour. Often this is because they don't understand the greatness of the real Jesus in the first place. Other times, it is because they don't want to follow Jesus. They want to make God according to their own image.

The same thing is true regarding the church. Some of us spend much of our time trying to change the church into something other than what it is. Granted, the church is in a constant state of development. This change is appropriate in the nonessential particulars of her adaptation to particular times and cultures.

Sometimes, however, it becomes painfully evident that some of her members don't like her essential character. Her essential character never changes. At this point it must be asked: If you don't like the church, why be a member? This may be painful to answer, but it is honest.

The same thing applies to the particular communities raised up by the Spirit in the church. Each community is unique. The charism of each is different. Yet they are all united by their common desire to live the gospel of Jesus. An individual must look honestly at the charismatic ideal and the experience of that ideal in practical daily life within the community to which they feel led by God. Does the community set a fire within their soul? Is the lifestyle of the community liveable? These questions must be answered before we can enter a community and persevere with integrity. Thank God, no one community has a monopoly on the work of the Spirit in the church!

Are we really called by God to a particular community? Do we really want to be members of the church? Do we really seek to follow Jesus, or do we really want to follow someone else? We are not above these things. We will never be above Jesus, the church he founded, or the communities raised up by his Spirit. If we want to be "above" these things, then these things are not for us. How do we wish to follow Jesus today?   □

The Road to Peace
John 14:1-6 (4:Friday)

Do not let your hearts be troubled. Have faith in God. **v. 1**

Jesus does not present peace as something that mystically permeates your soul as an unconditional gift from God. He presents it as a choice. It is a gift, but it must be responded to in order to be fully active in our life.

Peace is linked with faith. Faith is a decision and choice to believe in God. Sometimes this seems quite logical based on the objective facts. Sometimes it seems to go against all logic. Sometimes it goes against the almost overwhelming tide of public opinion or personal emotions. Yet the more we choose to have faith, the more peace we experience.

We will still experience conflict. Jesus emotionally broke in the Garden of Gethsemani. He wept at the death of his friend Lazarus. He grew angry when the disciples and the crowds did not understand his message. The peace of today's Gospel doesn't deny any of these very real and human emotions. It doesn't take them from our life. It simply helps us deal with them correctly.

Sometimes we lose our peace when we limit God to only one agenda or place. When he does it another way, we lose our peace. Paul tells us he will do more than "we can possibly expect or imagine" if we will just let go. We lose our peace when we limit God.

Lastly, the Gospel says Jesus is "the way, the truth, and the life." He says, "No one comes to the Father except through me." If we try to center any aspect of our life on anyone or anything but Jesus, we lose our peace. Sometimes these false centers are blatantly against God. Sometimes they are more subtle. They can even be good things, things that appear godly or Christian. Yet when we center on the thing and not on Jesus, we lose our peace.

Is your heart troubled today? Why? Do you choose to have faith? Do you limit God? Do you center on Jesus and Jesus alone? If you answer these three questions, you will be on the road back to peace. This is the message of today's Gospel. □

Can We Do Greater Works?
John 14:7-14 (4:Saturday)

The man who has faith in me will do the works I do, and greater far than these. v. 12

Do we do the works of Jesus? Perhaps we do not. Do we do even greater works? Perhaps we do. Ironically, both of these realities take place in our modern Christian life.

We often sell ourselves short of doing the literal works of Jesus. We read about them in the Gospels, but somehow we think them beyond us. Jesus could perform miracles, but not us! Jesus could preach powerfully, but not us. Jesus could do works of compassion and mercy, but not us.

This way of thinking is not correct. Jesus tells us that whatever we ask for in his name will be done if we really believe that what we ask for will happen. The apostles worked miracles, so have the saints throughout the ages.

What about us? Are we afraid to ask because we are humble, or because we are afraid we will fail and be humiliated? This is pride. We must be humble enough to obey. Then we will really do the works of Christ in our own lives.

On another level we do, in fact, perform even greater works than Jesus. Jesus lived in an insignificant conquered province of the Roman Empire. He was extremely limited regarding his direct effect upon his civilized world. He was poor. He could not vote. He enjoyed very few freedoms regarding basic human rights.

We are not in that situation. We live in the most powerful nation on the face of the earth. We enjoy a degree of basic human freedom unheard of ever before in human history. In many ways we can have a very tangible effect on our modern world. This happens on both a socio-economic and political level. Through our basic lifestyle choices as Americans, we have an effect on the rest of the world. This is a reality Jesus did not directly enjoy.

Still he was able to shake the civilized world. Despite his lack of basic human freedom, he had a faith that broke through all human barriers and set captives free throughout the rest of human history. Here, we still have much to learn. He was able to do so much with so little. We work with so much, yet the effect of our labors is still quite minimal.

Do we do the works of Christ? Do we do even greater works? We must be humble enough to believe and act in obedience. Then he will do great things that will continue to shake the world through you and me. □

Discerning God's Will
John 14:21-26 (5:Monday)

The Holy Spirit . . . will instruct you in everything, and remind you of all that I told you. v. 26

"God told me." So goes the justification of many of the sinful lifestyles among modern Christians. What is the balance between the heart and the mind, the subjective intuition and objective facts, in discerning the will of God?

It is true that the New Covenant is written primarily on the heart by the Spirit. It is this Spirit that teaches us and guides us. As St. John says, "The anointing you received from him remains in your hearts. This means you have no need for anyone to teach you. . . . that anointing taught you" (1 Jn 2:27).

Is this enough? Do we simply appeal to the teaching of the Spirit within to establish God's will regarding faith and morals? What happens when different people claim two clearly opposing "truths"?

This is where the rest of today's Gospel enters in. Jesus sent forth apostles to preach. He did not only send the Holy Spirit. These apostles themselves were given the Spirit in a special way to aid them in their task of leadership. Consequently, the church was given a twofold source of teaching: the Spirit and the apostles. The Spirit gave power. The apostles discerned. It was out of this twofold source of teaching authority that the Scriptures themselves were finally written and compiled, giving us yet a third: the Spirit, apostolic tradition, and the Scriptures. All three streams form one large river of life that guides us unto the truth of Jesus Christ.

How do we discern God's will in our life? Do we just rely on intuition of the Spirit, or are we also open to objective guidance from the church? Do we separate the Spirit, the church, and the Scriptures, or do we see them as one deposit of the apostolic faith? Learn to integrate. Then will you really see God's will. Then will your faith be Catholic, abundant, and full! □

A Peace Past Understanding
John 14:27-31 (5:Tuesday)

"Peace" is my farewell to you, my peace is my gift to you; I do not give it to you as the world gives peace. v. 27

How does the world give peace: through military control, political negotiation, or economic success on the corporate level; or external security and happiness on the private level? Both of these things are good, but they are not the peace that Jesus brings.

Jesus brings a peace that "passes all understanding." It is at work even in the midst of conflict and war. It is something internal, something of the Spirit. It can never be taken from us if we are living in the Spirit. Peace is a fruit of the Holy Spirit working within our soul. As St. Paul says, "The fruit of the Spirit is love, joy, peace" (Gal 5:22).

Where does the work of the Spirit go on?—in the heart and the mind. Before you can even say the word, "God," you must think it. As you direct your mind to certain thoughts, so will your heart follow. As Paul says, "Be transformed by the renewal of your mind" (Rom 12:2). He adds, "Your thoughts should be wholly directed ... Then will the God of peace be with you" (Phil 4:8-9). Isaiah said, "A nation of firm purpose you keep in peace; in peace, for its trust in you" (Is 26:3).

This brings us to peace of heart. St. Paul says, "Christ's peace must reign in your hearts, since as members of the one body you have been called to that peace" (Col 3:15). From the text we can see that they can have this peace because they first chose to "forgive," "love," and "thank." These things were all positive attitudes and choices that first had to be considered in the mind. Set your mind on the peace of God. Then your heart will follow.

Still this peace is not totally realized externally in the world. Paul says, "If possible, live peaceably with everyone" (Rom 12:18). The, "if possible," of that sentence is a big "if." There are still conflicts in this world. There are even conflicts in the church! It took both the religious and secular leaders to put Jesus to death. We still crucify Jesus in each other in the secular and religious arenas of our world. Despite all we might suffer, we must have the internal peace of Jesus that perseveres.

Do you know this peace in your life? If not, you might want to consider how well you control your thoughts. You want to see where your mind goes when it wanders. Does it go to God? Train your mind to meditate on God. Then it will wander back to him when it gets lost. Then you will know peace in your heart. □

Pruned Radishes
John 15:1-8 (5:Wednesday)

I am the true vine. v. 1

There are two lessons in today's Scripture: 1) Being radical for Christ and 2) Being pruned by Christ. We are all called to be radicals for Jesus, but what does "radical" mean? It means to be "rooted." Like a "radish"! It means that every aspect of our life must be firmly and surely rooted in Jesus and Jesus alone. Then our life will draw from the Author of life.

Radicals are not fanatics. The early church writing called the *Didache,* or *The Teaching of the Twelve Apostles,* said that fanaticism is a sin. What is a fanatic? A fanatic takes one particular aspect of radical living and emphasizes it to an absurd extreme. A good idea is pushed too far so that an extreme truth actually becomes error.

We are also called to the "pruning principle" by today's Gospel. What is the pruning principle? Trimming off the unfruitful branches of our life so that the fruitful ones will grow even stronger. Do we only prune the dead branches?

No, we do not. The branches to be pruned are filled with life, for they have an abundance of green leaves. But they do not bear abundant fruit. It would be easy if we only pruned off the dead branches. That is obvious. No. We must prune branches that appear to be alive, but they are not fruitful.

It is also significant how we are pruned. We are pruned by the word of God. The Book of Hebrews says that God's Word is sharper than a two-edged sword that separates even bone and marrow. The sword of the Word of God does prune. Do we really spend time meditating on his words so that they will prune us back to fruitful growth?

His word is not just in Scripture. It is also in religious superiors. It is incarnational. Jesus stood as a man in their midst. He does the same with us. Jesus comes to us in the church and our communities to proclaim his word. Do we allow ecclesial superiors to speak God's word to us? This is no longer just a matter of private interpretation. It is concrete and real. It deals with tangible areas of our life that are concretely dealt with by the help of another living and breathing person.

Pruning may be painful. Like the pruned branch, we may not always understand why we are being pruned. Yet if we allow the appropriate ministers to be Jesus to us, they will speak God's word in very tangible and concrete ways. We must trust that they really love us with the love of Christ.

We must also have faith that God works through even sinful superiors as long as they do not command against the church's teaching on faith or morality, or go against our particular community rule and constitutions. Superiors are quite human.

It takes supernatural faith for this to work. When it does, it helps to bring forth abundant fruit in our life that is very tangible. It is no longer a fuzzy and vague life, but is quite specific.

Do we have this faith? Are we willing to let Jesus prune us by his word that comes to us through the communities of the church? Is the life of our community rooted firmly in the gospel of Jesus? Are we ready to get specific as we become true radicals for Christ?   □

Out of the Pit
John 15:9-11 (5:Thursday)

Live on in my love. . . . that your joy may be complete. vv. 9, 11

Today we hear three basic concepts: love, obedience, and joy. We also move from self to selflessness, or self-sacrifice. Today we are invited to begin a process, to reach a life of love, truth, and joy.

First we must know that God loves us as nobody else can. No other human being on earth will love you as unconditionally as God. No matter how far we have fallen, no matter how dark the darkness, no matter how great the obstacle or sin, God loves us and offers us a way back to him. All we need to do is respond.

St. Bonaventure says that we are all like a person who has fallen into a deep, dark, and desperate pit. No matter how hard we try to climb out by our own power and plan, we will fail. We may get very high or even get right to the top. Still we are destined to slip and fall all the way back to the bottom as we rely upon ourselves. Most of us live our whole life going through this process over and over.

Bonaventure says that only Jesus can pull us up out of the pit. Jesus loves us so much that he reaches down to wherever we are in the depth or darkness of the pit. Then he will pull us up with his power and his plan. All we have to do is hold on.

Here we move from step one to step two. Here we move

from unconditional love to obedience to his truth. Here we move from coming to Jesus, "Just as I Am," to repentance and change. Here we move from Jesus' forgiveness of the woman caught in adultery, to his words, "Go your way and sin no more." This is the difference from the initial acceptance of God's love, to daily living on in God's love. It involves obedience to God's truth. This usually includes change.

This repentance leads us to new life. This change brings us to joy. Oh yes, changing our old habits and lifestyle patterns can be painful. The old self dies hard. Death is painful. But the rewards of joy are much greater, and they are eternal! As St. Francis said, suffering is short, joy is eternal. As Jesus said, "I came that they might have life and have it to the full" (Jn 10:10).

Will you take the steps to joy today? No matter where you are, allow God to love you. No sin is too great for God. Then allow his truth and his plan to lift you out of your pit. Then you will have joy. If you are sad in any area of your life today, take the steps to joy. Let Jesus lift you out of your pit.   ☐

Willing to Die?
John 15:12-17 (5:Friday)

There is no greater love than this: to lay down one's life for one's friends. v. 13

I often use the analogy of Jesus pushing a child out of the way of oncoming traffic and getting hit in the process to describe his substitutionary death on the cross for us. For me this is a very helpful analogy for people in the Western, modern world. The child may have been disobedient by going into the street. By cold, hard "justice" the child "deserved" to be hit. But Jesus sacrificed himself in order to save the child out of love.

This is a nice analogy. It uses a figure to which most of us can relate. But how many of us have ever seen the raw carnage of a traffic accident? Being hit by oncoming traffic often involves broken bones, compound fractures, torn flesh, exposed muscle, and an abundance of human blood. Put that usual image together with the screams and moans of accident victims, and you don't have a very pretty scene.

This is the reality of self-sacrificial love. Jesus says we must consider the cost of commitment before we make it. Likewise, before we get all warm and cuddly about "love," we had best consider what Jesus really meant. Christian love is not just a nice, warm, human emotion. It is a divine gift that empowers one to make supernatural human sacrifices. It causes us to do the extraordinary.

Paul says, "It is rare that anyone should lay down his life for a just man, though it is barely possible that for a good man someone may have the courage to die. It is precisely in this that God proves his love for us: that while we were still sinners, Christ died for us" (Rom 5:7-8). John says even further, "The way we came to understand love was that he laid down his life for us; we too must lay down our lives for our brothers" (1 Jn 3:16).

Are we willing to actually die for Jesus and for our brothers and sisters? Crucifixion is not pretty. The early Christians' death in the Roman arenas were not harmless sports spectacles. They both involved the painful reality of death. Are we ready to let go of everything, to die? This is the test of real love. □

The Name
John 15:18-21 (5:Saturday)

If you find that the world hates you, know it has hated me before you. . . . All this they will do to you because of my name. vv. 18, 21

Isn't it interesting how the world responds to Jesus' name? You can do something in the name of Buddha, or

Mohammed, even Krishna, and the world seems to tolerate it all quite well. Likewise, present a popular program and you're safe. Present only Jesus, and your "success" is in danger. Do something in Jesus' name, and literally all hell breaks loose! Why? Because all hell knows that he really has the power to chain the powers of the devil!

Buddha, Mohammed, or Krishna have not obtained the final truth that comes from God. Only Jesus is the way and the truth that leads to a life that is abundant and full. All others remain incomplete. As Scripture says, "at Jesus' name every knee must bend . . . and every tongue proclaim . . . JESUS CHRIST IS LORD!" (Phil 2:10).

This does not mean that all the world will automatically bow down and rise up to joyfully embrace the full truth of Jesus Christ. No. The war is between Satan and God. Jesus has won the victory. The battle's outcome is known, but Satan won't give up. Despite his defeat he keeps on battling. Until the full number of those who will believe in every age have given themselves to God, the Lord allows the battle to continue. Satan believes the battle to work against God, but God uses even the battle of the devil to strengthen the faith of the chosen followers of his Son.

This all means that many in this world who choose to follow the devil will continue to battle against God's saints. Jesus tells us they will treat us no better than they treated him. Just as with Jesus, they will think they have won the war by their persecution of us, but even in death we are the victors. The battle has already been won in Jesus' name.

According to early church teaching, there are three mysteries the devil did and does not know: the virgin birth, the resurrection, and the second coming. With the first two, he thought he had won through the slaughter of the innocents and the crucifixion. With the last, he believes he will be victorious with the rise of Antichrist in the world. With all three, the devil is wrong. Jesus is the victor. The battle is won.

Will you continue to fight the fight of Jesus even in the face of apparent defeat? Will you continue to stand for the way and name of Jesus, even when a compromise might seem the better way? Can you take the hatred of the world in order to obtain the love of God? If not, then you are not really a Christian. You have compromised the way of Jesus Christ. □

A Stable Spirit
John 15:26-16:4 (6:Monday)

I have told you all this to keep your faith from being shaken. v. 1

Why does Jesus tell us the things to come? So that as both the good and the bad come true, our faith will increase. Because he has told us at least some of the bad, when it does come true it will serve to strengthen, rather than destroy, our faith.

First he tells us the good news. We will be given the Holy Spirit. Why? So we can be witnesses even in the midst of the pain and suffering of this world. Yes, we will be given charismatic gifts to comfort the world's pain. But we are never promised that we will ever do away with all pain or never experience pain ourselves.

Today's Gospel promises, "Not only will they expel you from synagogues, a time will come when anyone who puts you to death will claim to be serving God." As we were told a few days ago, "They harm you as they harmed me. They will respect your words as they respected mine." This means we too might be mocked, persecuted, and even put to death for our witness of Jesus Christ.

We will not be powerless as we face this trial, though. We have been given a supernatural power. This power will not overcome all external opposition. This power will make us strong within. It will empower us to remain faithful to the teachings of Jesus even when it might seem humanly impossible. Jesus says to the disciples before Pentecost: "You will receive power when the Holy Spirit comes down on you; then you are to be my witnesses . . . even to the ends of the earth" (Acts 1:8).

How did the disciples give witness? By preaching, teaching, and working mercy and miracles? Yes. But even more by giving their life and remaining faithful even unto martyrdom.

Will we do the same? Is the gift of the Spirit nothing more

than a magician's trick for us? Or is it a matter of power to remain faithful to a whole way of life? If we know persecution will come, then it will not catch us off guard when it happens. It might happen in our lifetime. It might happen in our nation. It might even happen in our family and, God forbid, in our local church. Will you remain faithful when and if it comes? Ask for the real power of the Spirit. Then you will. ☐

The Paradox of Love
John 16:5-11 (6:Tuesday)

If I fail to go, the Paraclete will never come to you. v. 7

How is it that the deeper things of God come in paradoxes? What is a paradox? It is a seeming contradiction that remains true. So it is that the deeper truths of Christ teach us that lasting wealth only comes in poverty, true proclamation only comes with silence, and intimate communion only comes in solitude.

This is the main lesson of today's paradox: Our deepest union with Jesus can only come when he is physically gone. He is only really here when he is gone!

The mystery of the incarnation comes full circle in the ascension. First it is a mystery when the Triune Transcendent God, the One wholly other in self-sufficiency and beyond space and time, is wholly and perfectly revealed to humankind in the incarnation without diminishing either the Trinity or Transcendent Oneness of the Godhead. Next, the incarnation is only fully understood in the seeming absence of the ascension. This is because of the gift of the Spirit of Pentecost.

Why is it that only paradox can speak the deeper things of God to human beings? Because God is love and love is a mystery. Yes, love is a decision of the will that must be based upon fact. So it is that two lovers must objectively discern their compatibility before they consummate their union in marriage. But if love stays only in objective fact, then it is not love at all.

Love must permeate from the mind to the heart. It must go beyond objective fact to subjective feeling. It must go beyond decision to passion. Therefore, love is, to some degree, a mystery. It cannot be fully explained. If it relies solely on subjective feeling, it will fail for lack of objective decision when there is no apparent feeling at all. But if it never involves the objective fact, it is not love, nor is it really marriage. It is only an arrangement.

So it is that Jesus desires to marry us today. Yes, he wishes to give us objective discernment and guidance through a dialogue of truth in faith and morality. Then he wishes to go beyond these things and actually consummate his union with us through the subjective mystery of the passion. This is central to our faith. It is the paramount pivotal point of redemption. It is more than mere doctrine and theology. It is mystery. It is love union.

Do we allow God into the mystery of the heart? Do we stop him from consummating his union with us by trapping him in endless dialogue of theology and doctrine? Let Jesus take you beyond mere words to the overwhelming truth of union. Let him take you through the truth on to love. Then Jesus will be more than just a good idea. He will be your lover and your friend. He will be your Saviour. □

Prophetic Messages
John 16:12-15 (6:Wednesday)

I have much more to tell you, but you cannot bear it now. v. 12

Is everything we need to know about the Christian life contained in Scripture? Is it even contained in the words of

Christ? According to the words of Christ, it is not, at least not in the direct sense of the word.

There is a definite teaching authority in the church. The Spirit has been given to lead us unto all truth. Furthermore, the apostles were chosen and commissioned by Christ for leadership. Thus, there is an ongoing teaching authority that is given to the whole church collectively, each person individually, and the leadership as successors to the apostles.

To what does this ongoing teaching apply? Almost all of the major doctrines unique to Christianity developed in the post-apostolic era. Even many of the basic teachings of Saints Peter and Paul in the sub-apostolic era reflect a definite development in the faith and morality of the early church. As the church spread throughout the civilized world, it had to bring forth developed answers to the many specific challenges of each culture and time in a way that was still based in the simple gospel of Jesus Christ.

What are some of these modern issues? Pro-life, global poverty, nuclear arms, or the ecological crises are included. On the moral level, the issues threaten the very future of civilization as we know it.

The church teaches clearly on all these issues. The consistent life ethic is the thread that ties them all together. Pro-life fights the problems of sexual promiscuity and related issues such as abortion and the disintegration of the nuclear family. The right to private property and the communal dimension of all possessions answers the threat of global poverty. The teaching against the indiscriminate destruction of person or property prohibits the likes of nuclear or germ warfare. Lastly, the reverence for all human life and all life in general teaches us to protect the environment for the good of people and all forms of life.

Are we ready to take the simple teaching of Jesus as applied in a developed way through the church and bring it to the world? We have a prophetic message to bring. You find its seed in Scripture, its flow in the church, and its fruit is given freely to a hungry world. Do you have the courage to change your life and live according to the teachings of the church? She has the Spirit. She has the truth. The issues seem more than we can bear. Jesus and the church have an answer. Dare to live it. ☐

Living Examples
Matthew 28:16-20 (6:Thursday)

Go, therefore, and make disciples of all the nations. Baptize . . . teach . . . And know that I am with you always, until the end of the world! vv. 19-20

Jesus ascends to the Father in heaven, but he is not gone. He is still with us—through the church and through the Spirit. He will be with us until the end of the world, the second coming.

Jesus gives a special commission in today's Gospel. It is often called, "the great commission." To whom is it given? All believers? Yes and no. More properly, no and yes. It is given in a very specific way to the eleven. It is given to the apostles. They are given a special commission as those who were chosen by and lived with Jesus. They are the unquestioned leaders of the early church. It is to their authority that the first believers appealed when there were questions about faith and morality.

The apostles made sure that this authority was passed on so there would not be chaos and confusion in their absence. This was called apostolic succession. It was also the authority to which the early church appealed. It was out of this that a set of writings was compiled to give us a record of the earliest apostolic teaching. It was out of this apostolic authority that we were given our Scriptures.

This does not mean that the general promises of the great

commission are only for the leadership of the church. They are a symbol for us all. Specifically, we are told at the end of Mark's Gospel that many aspects of the apostolic charge are given to all who "profess their faith." We, too, are given an apostolic charge. How do we fulfill it?

The main way to preach is to live. Actions speak louder than words. Oh yes, there will be lay people given gifts by the Spirit for a particular task or ministry. But no extraordinary ministry is believable if it is not being lived. All of us are called to live Christianity before we preach it. Only then will the preaching, by ourselves or by others, be believed.

I am reminded of a point made by Billy Graham. He said that his preaching a crusade would be fruitless if the local Christians were not preaching by example of their lifestyles first. St. Francis said the same thing eight hundred years ago. He said preachers don't win souls. Simple people convert souls by their lifestyles and their prayers. In heaven they will obtain the reward for the conversion of souls before the preachers do.

Are you preaching with your lifestyle today? You can bet that you are. You either preach for Christ, or against, or anti-Christ. Who do you preach today? Also, how do you live in the church? Preaching is not something we do alone. We do it as a body, as a people. We preach together. How do you support the preaching of the church by your way of life? □

A Joyful Hope
John 16:20-23 (6:Friday)

*You will grieve for a time, but your grief will be turned to joy. . . .
On that day you will have no questions to ask me.* vv. 20, 23

Jesus was taken away from the disciples twice: on Good Friday and on Ascension Thursday, in the crucifixion and the ascension. Both events were followed by joy: on Easter

Sunday and at Pentecost, the resurrection and the giving of the Holy Spirit.

There is an "already" and a "not yet" implied in today's Gospel. On one level the joy is given by the Holy Spirit at Pentecost. On another level, even beyond the gift of the Spirit, our final joy is only at the end of this age at the second coming. This will usher in the joy that is complete as we see the Father face-to-face with Jesus Christ and the Holy Spirit.

This is brought out further by the letter of St. Paul to the Romans in his great "Spirit chapter," chapter eight: "Although we have the Spirit as first fruits, we ourselves groan inwardly while we await the redemption of our bodies. In hope we are saved. But hope is not hope if its object is seen." Therefore, both salvation and redemption are "already and not yet." Pentecost has come already. The second coming still remains.

This means there is a tension even for most "Spirit-filled" Christians in today's world. We still have days when it seems that Jesus has left us again. Sometimes he seems far away. It is like a husband who loves you intimately through the night, stays with you at the beginning of the morning, and then leaves to support the family during the day. We sometimes feel quite alone as we do our job of raising the children of the family while our husband is away. Important as our job may be as "Mother Church," we sometimes feel abandoned and ignored. Do not fear. Jesus returns at the end of the day. He will love us again in a gentle embrace.

Likewise, our children will grow into fine men and women of God if we do our job well. These are both reasons for hope and joy.

How well do you deal with your times of sorrow? Do you sometimes feel abandoned by Christ or unappreciated by the physical or spiritual children you raise in the church? Do not despair. Jesus told us this time would come. The question is: Will you respond with faith, hope, and charity, or will you lose virtue and joy? ☐

Live Simply as Some Simply Live
John 16:23-28 (6:Saturday)

Ask and you shall receive, that your joy may be full. v. 24

Many Christians believe that if you are not sober and somber, you are not holy. This is true in many peace and social justice circles. It is also true among those who think themselves contemplatives.

However, some of the most deeply committed people I have ever met personally in both of these areas have also been some of the most joyful. The contemplatives do not walk around with head bowed and speaking in hushed tones all of the time. Nor do the peace and social justice activists see a devil behind every joy. No. Those who are most mature in both of these valid aspects of Christianity have also learned how to enjoy to the full the simple pleasures God has given us.

I have often quoted Ghandi, "Live simply so that others may simply live." He himself was only saying what St. Augustine and St. Francis said long before him: Whatever you indulge of your wants, you steal from the poor. Or as I say: Differentiate between your wants and your needs, for habitually indulging your wants is killing the needy.

Does this mean God never wants us to enjoy ourselves? Absolutely not! God wants to meet our needs and wants us to enjoy having our needs met. He even wants to indulge our wants from time to time and to enjoy and relax in doing so.

For example, I like an occasional frozen yogurt. Is it a need? No it is not, but I do not believe God is offended. Nor do I believe my simple lifestyle is in jeopardy. Only if I began to demand it daily and consider it a "need" would I be in real moral trouble.

The problem is that the minority of the world is still rich, while the majority are desperately poor. Furthermore, the rich are getting richer, while the poor are getting poorer. The habitual indulgence of wants by the few is depriving the many of their basic needs. This cannot go on. It takes the gift from God and mocks it. It abuses a good thing and turns it into sin.

Do we find joy in the basic gifts from God? Do we find joy in the simple pleasures of life, such as having our needs met by God or enjoying a little surprise or unexpected gift? If we do not, then chances are we have lost our real appreciation of the more important gift of life. □

When the Going Gets Tough, Stay
John 16:29-33 (7:Monday)

"You will be scattered . . . leaving me quite alone. (Yet I can never be alone; the Father is with me.) I tell you all this that in me you may find peace. vv. 32-33

How well do we handle solitude? Oh yes, it is easy when our solitude is a place of our own choosing, for a chosen length of time. What about the solitude that is beyond our control? What about the solitude of loneliness or desertion? This is more like the solitude of today's Gospel.

Jesus is foretelling that those closest to him will deny and desert him. Those who ate with him, lived with him, and saw him most intimately would deny him when the going got tough. He would be left to face Calvary alone. Yet, he is not alone. His Father is with him. Therefore, everything is under control.

We, too, face our Calvary of forced solitude. We, too, experience the absence of those closest to us in times when we need them the most. We experience the loss of a loved one in sickness and death. We experience the tragedy of separation and divorce. Furthermore, the very transience of Western society makes it difficult to maintain the healthy bonds of any close relationship. People come and people go. It is a sad reality in modern life.

We have seen this in intentional Christian community. Over a period of ten years we have seen many people come and go. At times it felt like our community was a revolving door. We found that it is very difficult for Americans to make a commitment and stick to it. In the end most will not. What is the answer?

There are two initial reactions and one response. The reactions are extreme. The response is moderate. One reaction says to bend with the trend of society and make binding and permanent commitments obsolete. The other reaction says to dig in deeper and just insist on them more strongly.

We have found a response that provides a third way. We provide graduation of time periods and states of life that allow a person to pass through a series of temporary commitments towards a permanent commitment. We also allow a single state of life that allows temporary commitment with the option of permanence. Even with this accommodation, we find many who do not live up to their commitment. Many people still come and go.

I have been in Switzerland for a few days. I have seen their mountain villages where family names are written on the side of old chalets, and churchyard graves are kept and groomed regularly by family members. I am reminded that the normal state of the world was a simple and stable way of life where families stayed in one local area for centuries. Only our century has seen the shift to radical transience. I am not so sure it is good.

Our first response to this must be twofold: rebuild Christian communities that re-establish this simplicity and stability in the midst of and as an alternative to this transient and materialist world. Second, learn to deal with the forced absences and desertions by finding our greater stability and friendship in God. He will not desert us. He will not leave us alone. He is with us always, even to the end of the world. □

Heart to Heart
John 17:1-11 (7:Tuesday)

Eternal life is this: to know you, the only true God, and him whom you have sent, Jesus Christ. v. 3

This sounds so simple! So it is. In simplicity we can see many theological truths in today's Gospel that have radical and tangible effects on our religious and secular life.

First, it implies that those who are not overtly "Christian" might still have eternal life. The church clearly teaches that while the fullness of God's revealed truth is only found in Christ, those who, through no fault of their own, have never heard the message of Jesus Christ presented in the power of the Spirit, yet still seek after the truth of God in sincerity and faith, will be saved. This radically affects the way we approach those of other faiths. It causes us to be bold in presenting the fullness of truth in Christ to them, yet with a humble respect for the very real aspect of truth that is revealed through their religion. It gives us both boldness and humble respect.

For Christians this Gospel tells another story. There is a call to a truth that is living experience rather than just a cold, objective fact. Today we are called to "know" Jesus Christ. This word, "know," is also used to describe the sexual intercourse between husband and wife, such as in "Adam 'knew' Eve." Therefore, to "know" Jesus is not just to intellectually assent to his Lordship in your life, even though this intellectual assent is part of "knowing" Jesus. To fully "know" Jesus is to go beyond objective truth and dogma and fully enter into and consummate mystical union with Christ. This is done through the death and resurrection, the passion of Jesus.

Do we allow this "passion" in our relationship with Jesus, or do we leave it on a purely objective level of intellectual assent? Do we even look beyond the doctrinal differences of the mind between various religions and look to the heart of their faith? I am not proposing a total disregard for doctrinal truth. It is an important part of the faith. I only recommend we keep it in its proper place. The New Covenant is written primarily on the heart.

Let him write his law on your heart then let him take care of your mind. Then you will find that Jesus can begin to break down the human and doctrinal barriers that still stand between sincere and faithful seekers and worshipers of the one true God. □

Sidetracked Vision
John 17:11-19 (7:Wednesday)

These are in the world . . . I do not ask you to take them out of the world, but to guard them from the evil one. They are not of the world, any more than I belong to the world. vv. 11, 15, 16

Be in the world, but not of the world. So it has been said over and over to Christians who struggle with the mundane realities of raising a family, developing a career, or simply maintaining a household and its incumbent responsibilities. It has also become the byword for all those who try to justify their worldliness and materialism as Christians. Where do we draw the line?

St. John speaks of "worldliness," when he says, "Have no love for the world, nor the things the world affords. If anyone loves the world, the Father's love has no place in him, for nothing that the world affords comes from the Father. Carnal allurements, enticements of the eye, the life of empty show—all these are from the world. And the world with its seductions is passing away" (1 Jn 2:15-17).

Such a list is somewhat different than St. Paul's list of "carnality." Paul says: "It is obvious what proceeds from the flesh: lewd conduct, impurity, licentiousness, idolatry, sorcery, hostilities, bickerings, jealousy, outbursts of rage, selfish rivalries, dissensions, . . . orgies, and the like. I warn you, as I have warned you before: those who do such things will not inherit the kingdom of God!" (Gal 5:19-21). This list is bad enough, when read in its completeness! We are guilty of such things from time to time and demand immediate repentance so as to stay in full union with God. But worldliness is something even more subtle.

I write this from a four-day excursion in Switzerland during the recordings of a Christmas project in London. There are two ways to see Switzerland: to get caught up in the expensive food and lodgings or the many high priced items available in all tourist areas; or to simply relax and drink in the wonder of God in his creation. The Swiss Alps are truly breathtaking! I will keep the memories of mountain pastures filled with wildflowers, sheer cliffs and snow-covered peaks, and quaint mountain villages long after the frills of the trip are gone. The same is true with most places and things in my life.

What about our daily life? Do we get sidetracked in that which is passing away, and miss that which will endure forever? We must all live in the world. All of us, even in communities and monasteries, must pay bills and coordinate ministries and industries. All of us must feed and clothe ourselves and provide shelter. But how do we do this? Do we see through creation to the Creator, or do we get stuck in a creation that is passing away? If we look for the Creator in everything, we will come to truly appreciate the created in a way that brings forth a simple lifestyle free of worldliness. If we get stuck in the creation without the Creator, we will become materialistic, worldly in our outlook, and horribly incomplete as a human being.   □

Credible Witnesses
John 17:20-26 (7:Thursday)

That all may be one . . . that the world may believe that you sent me. v. 21

Christians are not united. The world does not believe. This is a sad indictment upon our witness, but unfortunately it is true.

Unity is not some kind of ecumenical beast out to gobble up orthodoxy. Nor is it an exercise in building one's own church persuasion into an all controlling empire. It is a matter of obedience to the Word of Jesus Christ. It is also a matter of credibility before a watching world.

How does Jesus give unity? He does it through the Spirit and through truth. On the level of objective truth, Jesus himself is the way, the truth, and the life. He himself chose the apostles in union with Peter and commissioned them to preach his truth to the world. They, in turn, established successors to their ministry so that a certain apostolic succession spread throughout the world. When there was a question about truth, it was to this apostolic succession that the early church appealed. From this process came the Scriptures themselves. Thus, the authority of the Scriptures builds on the authority of the church established by God. If you deny the authority of the early church, you end up destroying the authority of the Scriptures, no matter how frequently or ardently you appeal to them.

Today, if there is a particular controversial passage of Scripture that is dividing the church (and there are many), it only makes sense to go back to the church from which we got the Scripture to see if they have at least a substantial agreement in interpretation as to what that passage of Scripture means. Then, you find all of the essential doctrines of Catholicism already in place, at least in their primitive expression in the early church. You also see that these doctrines are all centered squarely on Jesus and Jesus alone.

There is much greater unity than that of church structure and doctrine, however. It is the doctrine of Spirit. I can be united structurally and doctrinally with a Catholic, but still be disconnected in the Spirit. Likewise, I can be disconnected in structure and doctrine with a Protestant, but be united in Spirit. If I choose between the two, I definitely choose the latter as the greater and most gratifying unity, though I admit that neither unity is really complete.

God wants our unity to be like the "body of Christ." It has a body, a soul, and a spirit. The body is structure. The soul or mind is doctrine. And the spirit is the Holy Spirit.

Let us pray for the day that the various levels of unity now enjoyed between professing Christians will grow to completeness. Let us begin within our own church and work outward. Let us begin person-to-person and then proceed church-to-church. Let us do so, not so much to build our church, but to give credible witness of Christ to the world. □

Productive Pain
John 21:15-19 (7:Friday)

A third time Jesus asked him, "Simon, son of John, do you love me?" Peter was hurt because he had asked a third time, "Do you love me?" So he said to him, "Lord, you know everything. You know well that I love you." Jesus said to him, "Feed my sheep." v. 17

How well do we respond to our times of penance? Real repentance demands not only a heartfelt turning back to God, but a reconciliation accomplished by achieving a certain justice. As St. John the Baptist says, "Bring forth works of repentance." This is what Jesus walks Peter through in today's Gospel.

Peter had denied Jesus three times. In this his sin was no less and perhaps even greater than that of Judas. Peter's sorrow led him to repent where Judas' sorrow led only to despair and suicidal death. This was Peter's salvation.

It is not quite as easy as the words sound. Peter had to come face-to-face with the same Jesus he had denied three times. He couldn't just pretend like nothing had happened. They both knew well his sin. There had to be reconciliation through painful honesty and confession. Because Peter had denied Jesus three times, Jesus makes Peter admit his love for him three times. This is very loving, but it is also very just. No doubt, it was also painful for Peter.

We too must be led through the same process if our repentance is to be truly life-giving, rich, and full. This means that we too must begin with a painfully honest inventory of our life and humbly confess our sins. As St.

James says, this must be to another person, and to a church leader if possible.

Jesus would go further and commend us to confess to the person we have offended when possible. We must ask forgiveness and state our willingness to change. Then we must make good the damage we have done if we can. If we cannot do all this, then we must bear the pain of a relationship that is only partly reconciled, even though we are ready to forgive, make good, and continue on.

Only after Peter has gone through this process personally is he ready to teach and minister to others. Granted, he was given the power of the keys upon his confession of faith in Jesus as the Christ. But only after he had personally been through backsliding and reconciliation could he minister to others with real understanding. Peter might well have been the leader of the apostolic church, but this experience kept him from conceit. He would always be a forgiven sinner, ministering God's forgiveness to others.

Do we minister from our own experience of Christ, or do we minister and teach from mere theory? To go through the process may be painful, but it is only through this pain of confession, repentance, and reconciliation that we can really know God's comfort and give that comfort to others. Do not be afraid of the pain. Then you will gain much. Try to avoid the pain and you will gain nothing. ☐

Major and Minor Concerns
John 21:20-25 (7:Saturday)

"Suppose I want him to stay until I come," Jesus replied, "how does that concern you? Your business is to follow me." v. 22

There are many theories about the end times nowadays. Some expect the coming of Jesus at any time. Some go so far as to get very specific about the time and circumstances. Every generation that has seen a serious renewal of the

Spirit has seen similar expectations, but any expectation that begins setting precise dates and times on the Lord's return is bordering on serious theological and pastoral trouble. Today's Gospel gives us some helpful pointers in the midst of our own troubled time.

Jesus at least hints that it is possible for the apostle John to remain alive until the second coming. Needless to say, this created quite a stir among the first Christians. Even after the report of John's death at Ephesus, many speculated that John was still alive and traveling the world. Still today you find a few who actually believe that John still walks the earth. Such beliefs come from an erroneous emphasis on the words of Christ and leave the more important issues unheeded.

Jesus says, "Suppose I want him to stay until I come. How does that concern you? Your business is to follow me." Our business is not to speculate about the precise details of the end times. Our business is to follow Jesus completely. If we do that, then the end times will take care of themselves.

I use an axiom to guide me in all of this: if you are ready to stay, then you are ready to go; if you are ready to go, then you are ready to stay. This means I must be willing to bear the responsibility of all my actions and words while still on this earth. I can only act properly on this earth if I am disposed of any attachment to earthly things by keeping my lasting hope in heaven and heaven alone.

Are we ready to either stay or go? Have we set our sights on the important things, or the unimportant? Have we really made it our business to radically follow Jesus Christ, or do we get sidetracked by unimportant and useless speculation? Major on the majors, and minor on the minors. Jesus is the Major. Center on him, and the minors will take care of themselves. □

Special Introductory Offer

NEW COVENANT

The Magazine of Catholic Renewal

Month by month, *New Covenant* will bring you inspiration, teaching, and personal testimony that will help you:

- deepen your prayer life
- better understand your Catholic faith
- live as a Christian in today's world

Just write to the address below for a free copy of *New Covenant.* If you like what you see, pay the invoice and you'll receive eleven more copies—one year of *New Covenant* for only $14.95.

NEW COVENANT
Department S
P.O. Box 7009
Ann Arbor, MI 48107

Other Books in This Series
by John Michael Talbot

Reflections on the Gospels
Volume One

Daily meditations on various readings from the Gospels that reveal much of what motivated John Michael Talbot to abandon all in order to follow Christ and live a simple life, marked by obedience, poverty, and humility. Containing approximately four months of daily meditations, *Reflections on the Gospels, Volume One* speaks of our need to have faith, to be honest about our failings, and to put everything we have in the hands of Christ. *$6.95*

Reflections on the Gospels
Volume Two

This companion edition to Volume One contains approximately four additional months of daily meditations on various readings from the Gospels. Talbot continues to call all Christians to live radically for Christ. His concise, to-the-point reflections will challenge Christians to examine the depth and quality of their response to that gospel. *$6.95*

Available at your Christian bookstore or from:
Servant Publications • Dept. 209 • P.O. Box 7455
Ann Arbor, Michigan 48107
Please include payment plus $1.25 per book
for postage and handling.
Send for our FREE catalog of Christian
books, music, and cassettes.